Searching for
Harry Chapin's America

Advance Praise for *Searching for Harry Chapin's America: Remember When the Music*

"The perfect marriage of author and subject. Fenton doesn't just trace the roots of Harry Chapin's music, he dares to explore the American soul, extracting from it much of the pulmonary essence that made Chapin such a classic American troubadour. By illuminating the physical and spiritual landscape of Chapin's artistry as a songwriter and voice of the common American, Fenton delivers a gem. Get this book, read it, and pass it on to someone you care about."
    —T. J. English, *New York Times* bestselling author

"Patrick Fenton has written a unique appreciation of a musical artist's work by going on tour in the footsteps of Harry Chapin and listening to the American Everyman tell the other half of this timeless troubadour's wonderful story-songs. In the clear, beautiful prose of a blue-collar scribe, Fenton records the thumping heartbeat of the American heartland that keeps the music and stories of Harry Chapin alive, decades after his death."
    —Denis Hamill, author of *Fork in the Road*

"Harry and Pat were made for one another. This is no vapid tell-all; no, it's a painstaking account of Harry's most important gift to us— his songs. Pat has a rare gift for getting to the roots and ruminations of musicians and their music. And as I read, I'm transported back to a lovely July evening in Central Park, the sweet and sour smell of pot rising above a huge crowd, as each of us awaits the defining line of 'Taxi,': 'We'd both gotten what we asked for such a long, long time ago.' We did indeed. We got Harry. And he's back in all his urgency and piquant curiosity in the pages of this wonderful book."
    —Larry Kirwan, writer/musician/lead singer for Black 47

"As we say in our neighborhood about Chapin, 'he pulled everybody's covers.' Chapin always went for truth. Pat Fenton's book nails that Chapin was a full dimensional dude. He didn't always make life (through his songs) feel like a sunny day. But Pat Fenton's gets Chapin's complexity and lets us know there are always many ways to look at things."
    —Brian Hamill, photojournalist

Searching for Harry Chapin's America

Remember When the Music

PAT FENTON

Heliotrope Books
New York

For Patricia ("the good looking Pat"),
my wife, my best friend, who was always
by my side with advice and love as this
book took form.
Thanks for being you.

Contents

New York State

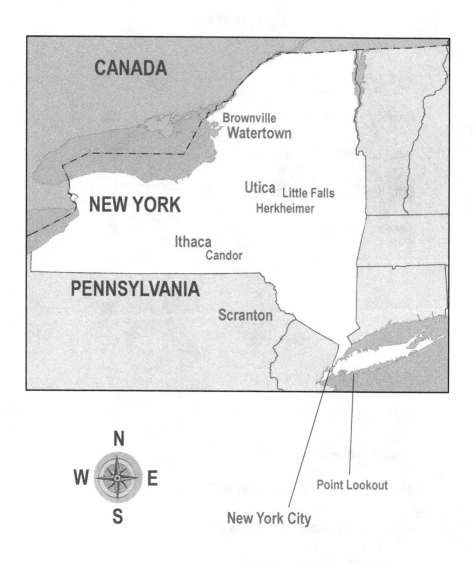

CANADA

Brownville
Watertown

Utica Little Falls
Herkheimer

NEW YORK

Ithaca
Candor

PENNSYLVANIA

Scranton

N
W E
S

Point Lookout

New York City

The Road Trip
of the search for Harry Chapin's America

The Big Picture

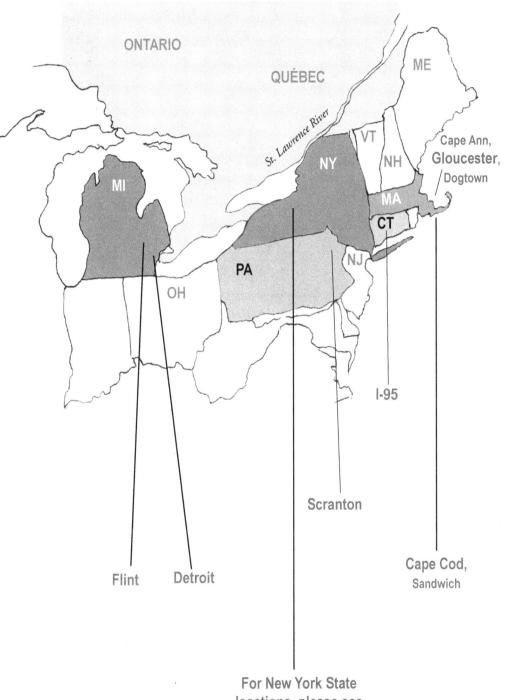

ONTARIO

QUÉBEC

ME

St. Lawrence River

VT

NY

NH

Cape Ann,
Gloucester,
Dogtown

MI

MA

CT

PA

NJ

OH

I-95

Scranton

Flint   Detroit

Cape Cod,
Sandwich

For New York State
locations, please see
opposite page

Introduction

"He had a huge audience of people that felt that he was singing for them, people who felt left out of the picture. He was a tremendous songwriter and storyteller."

—David Amram

"Harry may have seen some little guy drinking at the bar. That's all he needed... Then he just made up the rest of the story. The key thing was that he got into the hearts and minds of average people. And also, not just average people, but sometimes people who were troubled, to say the least. And then he just created their stories. Remember the genre was called story songs."

—Bill Ayres

The first time I ever heard a Harry Chapin song, I was driving an empty New York City yellow cab down Central Park West at midnight in winter—the dark street and doormen hailing cabs in a blur before me, my foot so hard on the pedal that I thought I might fly. I was heading home via a cab company called Ike Stan in Long Island City. This was 1972, when the song "Taxi" first came out, and I could not have been situated more perfectly to hear it on the radio.

Every now and then in America, an original voice like Harry Chapin's comes along. He belongs up there with Bruce Springsteen, Don McLean, Joni Mitchell, Janice Ian, and Billy Joel. And in his own way, Chapin did with cello what Bob Dylan did with harmonica; he forged a style of music we had never quite heard before.

Once asked by an interviewer to describe his style of music, Chapin said, "It's sort of interesting because it's after folk has happened, it's after rock. It's a throwback, especially in the longer songs, to an older ballad form ... I'd like to come up with some answer to that, but it's hard." While fresh, contemporary, and informed by rock idioms, Harry's genre can be traced back to the roots of early American folk music, a kind of storytelling through ballad.

Harry might never have known the extent to which he gave live audiences the sense that he was living in many of the songs he sang, long after he exited the stage and went home. He left them with the feeling that his songs were who he was, who they were. Although Harry Chapin became a star, he never got rid of the "everyman" quality that drove his music. Still, after all the years since his death in 1981, little has been published about that wonderful eye he had on our small towns and cities—how he could capture, in song lyrics, the very sinew of American life and all its drama. I started to wonder about his legacy, not only on Long Island, but also throughout New York City and America. The importance of who he was and what he wrote did not seem to be getting out there enough.

Back in 2000, I hosted a live late night radio show called "Night Thoughts" on WGBB, a small station on Long Island. I used to play his song "WOLD" for my opening. Eventually, I invited his daughter Jen as a guest on the show and stayed in touch with her. A few months later, after reading some of my work, she asked if I would be interested in writing a book about her father.

Thus began my Harry Chapin odyssey. Juggling my own career, teaching, writing plays and articles for New York papers like the *New York Times*, the *Daily News*, and *Newsday*, and hosting the radio show, I worked on the book on and off for nearly twenty years. Something kept pulling me back to it. What really surprised me then, and still does, is that there weren't already ten books on him.

I envisioned my book as a long conversation with people who, for one reason or another, either fan or family, had a connection with Harry. Through Jen, I met her mother, Sandy Chapin, on a rain-soaked night in Northport, Long Island. Sandy and I went to Gunther's Bar, a blue-collar saloon on Main Street, to talk about her late husband. It's fitting that the bar is where Jack Kerouac, another great American writer, hung out.

I ordered Sandy a Chardonnay, but unfortunately, there was none to be had in Gunther's in 2000. I couldn't even get her "any old white wine." It felt as if I was asking for some rare vintage, available only in France. A glass of white Zinfandel finally emerged, and the two of us moved over to a corner next to the front windows while a band played covers by Hank Williams. Over that cheap wine and a few pints of beer, gazing at the emptiness of Main Street as rain poured down, we spoke of my book about Harry.

We immediately agreed that it would not be an official biography or a tome about his life in music. We hoped for the resonance of William Least Heat-Moon's book, *Blue Highways, A Journey Into America*, which we both loved. As in Heat-Moon, we decided, I would be on the road, talking to everyday people. I wanted to walk inside the lyrics of Harry's songs by visiting some of the places where they happened and talking to some of the people who made up the America he was singing about.

Many whom I would meet on Harry's road—people in bus depots, diners, and small-town saloons—spoke like they had indeed walked out of his lyrics. Many looked it, too. From bartenders to bowling alley patrons, they described, in their own words, what they thought his music was about. And they did it better than I could in a formal biography, which is why I am sharing these encounters here.

I never forgot racing that empty, yellow cab down Central Park West, as I listened to "Taxi," and loved the lyrics where

Harry sings: "I stashed the bill in my shirt." In those days, you weren't really a New York City cab driver unless you stashed some bills, or could say that you wolfed down a fifteen-minute meal of meatloaf and mashed potatoes served up from a steam table at the old Belmore Cafeteria down on 28th Street. The place would be full all night long with old Jewish drivers, some just starting their night, some ending it. They sat around drinking mugs of coffee and telling stories with the ease of standup comics. They're all gone now. That was another New York. Later, Martin Scorsese's film *Taxi Driver* would catch the black and white New York City grit of the Belmore Cafeteria and make it famous.

Rumor has it that the screenplay for *Taxi Driver* was inspired by Chapin's "Taxi," which had come out a few years earlier, an anthem for that legion of New York cab drivers who hung out at the old Belmore—despite "Taxi" having been set in San Francisco. There is certainly a creative connection between the two works, some sort of longing by the characters in the song and the film for an unreachable, better life.

Harry never did drive a cab, but when he was down and out at age 28, he did go to the New York City Taxi and Limousine Commission at 87 Beaver Street and file for a hack license. "My daughter Jennie is six months on the way to being born, and I panic. I set into New York City to sign up for a hack license," he described at the time. He was in and out of jobs; at one point he was a bank teller. With a new baby on the way, he assessed that driving a cab didn't seem so bad. I'm not sure why he never went through with it.

The song "Taxi" came to him one day as he was riding into New York City on the Long Island Railroad and read a wedding announcement. An ex-girlfriend who lived up in Scarsdale was marrying a rich businessman. As Harry looked down at her image in the *New York Times*, the song started coming to him. A combination of that photograph, and his hack license, inspired it. As the train rocked into Pennsylvania Station, lyrics were still pouring out of him. Surrounded by commuters off to their

9-to-5 gigs in the offices of the city, this unknown guy with the tumbling, curly hair and the crew neck sweater was writing his way into fame.

"...and she glanced at the license for my name,
a smile seemed to come to her slowly,
It was a sad smile, just the same.
And she said, How are you, Harry?
I said, How are you, Sue? Through the too many miles And the
too-little smiles I still remember you..."

The old girlfriend's name was Claire, not Sue. She would be into her second marriage after Harry died. His daughter Jen would grow up and become a singer herself, and chairwoman of World Hunger Year's board of directors. Harry co-founded World Hunger Year, a New York-based nonprofit aiming to end hunger and poverty, with Bill Ayres in 1975. Today, it is called WHYHunger.

I started to spend some time with Harry's family and close friends, the people who knew his true north, his hopes, his dreams, his troubles. Then I went out on the road to search for what is left, if anything, of the America in his songs. In no particular chronological order, I drove the same roads he did, using his songs as my map. Leaving Cape Cod, for example, I drove over the Sagamore Bridge and picked up Route 3, to Cape Ann in Gloucester, to Dogtown. I crossed the width of Massachusetts in two-and-a-half hours to get to the upper parts of New York State, my destination being Watertown, not far from the edge of Canada. Up there in the cold country, Harry Chapin had once stopped into a bar and walked out with the idea for his song "A Better Place to Be."

Harry's relatives and close friends all had a story about the last day he lived and where they were when they learned of his death on the Long Island Expressway. I would bring the question up to them as gently as I could, and then later, after transcribing their interviews and hearing these stories again on tape over a glass of scotch, I decided to leave much of that part out. It was too sad.

When Harry died, we lost the voice of someone who had the rare talent of defining a part of America in his lyrics—a living, breathing, seemingly unremarkable part of it that most of us miss as we rush through life. From as far upstate in New York as Watertown to all over Long Island and Brooklyn too, you can still hear folks tell Harry Chapin stories about how his songs helped them get through the night. I wanted to seek out those voices. It's all part of the long, unwritten story about who Harry Chapin really was, and how much he is missed.

In the end, I realized he was his songs.

Remembering Harry With Bill Ayres

"I remember reading this book some years ago where the author had this line that just knocked me over: 'We tell our stories to live.' ... Harry... said, 'Yeah. That's right, absolutely right.' And the notion was that everyone has a story inside of them. And he recognized that."

—Bill Ayres

In 1991 I delivered a lecture on Harry Chapin's life at Queensborough College. I was teaching a course on creative writing at night, and this two-hour presentation was about what we lost on that summer night ten years earlier, in 1981.

A priest I knew, Monsignor Tom Hartman, told me about Bill Ayres, the former priest who founded World Hunger Year with Harry Chapin. To prepare for my lecture about Chapin's life, Father Tom helped me set up an interview with Ayres.

One fall afternoon, I headed up to the Garment District in Manhattan where the headquarters of World Hunger Year was located. James Chapin, Harry's oldest brother, would join us for the interview. I brought along my exhaustive list of questions, and I was grateful for the patience that Ayres and James exhibited in their candid and honest answers. They left me with the impression that Harry Chapin's talent, his beauty as a human being, was so rare that you had to include his weaknesses to fully understand him. It's been over 25 years since I conducted that interview, but it's a fitting place to start a story about him. As Shakespeare said, "what's past is prologue."

PF: Bill, do you think that the relationship that Harry had with his stepfather, which was at times not always an easy one, inspired him to write some of the darker themes that showed up in his story songs?

BA: Yeah, but I think something else came through, and that is Harry's identification with the underdog, Harry's identification with the little guy, with the person that is struggling to make some sort of sense out of the craziness of their life. And finding some sort of meaning. Harry could get inside those experiences. He could find the experiences first of all, get inside them and make them magical, so that you entered into those experiences with him. They were stories and as you heard the story, a part of it was the story of your life. That was part of Harry's magic. He was a wonderful storyteller.

PF: How did he avoid passing along to his own children the mean-spiritedness he experienced?

BA: He decided that he was going to break the cycle. If there was one thing that Harry Chapin was not, that's mean-spirited. He was not a violent person. He was a person who had been hurt. No doubt about that. And he had a great desire to help to heal. That's why he did the music: To heal himself, first of all (*laughs softly*). And then to help heal other people. And that's why he got involved in hunger. That's why he got involved in some of the causes that he felt so strongly about.

PF: A lot of his songs have a dark side to them. Is that one of the reasons that he didn't get on the air as much?

Harry's older brother, James Chapin, walks into the room and Bill

Ayres introduces me to him. James jumps in right away and takes the question.

JC: I remember his first album had this nine-minute song about a drug addict, and the second one had a ten-minute song about a sniper (*laughs*).

James goes on to talk about Claire MacIntyre, an old girlfriend of Harry's who he called "Sue" in his song, "Taxi."

JC: Harry had this violent relationship with Claire MacIntyre, the girl he wrote "Taxi" for. One night, the two of them got so mad at each other that she screeched the car to a halt, and they both jumped out and started hollering at each other in front of a bar in the middle of Harlem. And she got so mad at him she stomped his foot with a high heel and broke some of the bones (*laughing*). And all the black guys in this bar came out and they were cheering them on. They thought that it was the greatest damn thing. They were hollering, "Go, go!" They thought it was funny seeing these two white, preppy types hollering at each other. He didn't even realize it until he got back in the car, but she had actually broken his middle toe by stomping on it with her spiked heel.

Harry found it very hard to get mad. And he was totally non-physically mad. I don't think that I ever saw him really, really mess up. I never saw him lose his temper basically in our whole relationship. So, he was not a very angry person that way. But he wrote about it a lot.

PF: It seems to me that some of the stuff that got into his songs was his version of a reworked Norman Rockwell image of life that he had in his head. He seemed optimistic.

BA: Yeah, but he was also interested in the dark side.

JC: Some of his songs were very glum. Especially his last album. I mean the first time our brother Tommy heard it he said, "It was very glum." And remember a lot of these things come from his autobiography, like "Burning Herself" and "They Called Her Easy."

Harry sometimes said that one of the ways that you can deal with dark things is to get it outside by writing about it. Remember that famous *Twilight Zone* episode on television when the monster is following the writer around and finally he says, "We're your private demons"? So you get it outside by writing about it.

BA: Anything was grist for the mill for Harry. So it wasn't just that he was going inside of himself, but he would see something out there and he would connect with it. And then he would take it for a ride.

JC: He had this little notebook and he would write down every damn thing that happened in it. So if he had to write something, a lot of times what he would do is, he would flip it open and start looking through the book. And he had all these kind of odd snatches of life in there.

The Johnson O'Connor testing institute actually did a test of him once. That was when Claire's father wanted him to take it. He said, "Okay, let's see what he's good at." They did a full day of testing. And it wasn't just written testing. They did oral testing too.

They do tests about your tuning pitch. They do tests about your facility with putting things together. They have a very interesting idea at that institute, which is that people are defined not by their capacities but their incapacities. In other words, you can't be good at some things unless you're not good at other things.

For example, I could not be, say, a historian if I really wanted to have a lot of physical exercise. You cannot be a good historian because you couldn't sit around all day. So, I'm perfectly made to sit all day and read. In other words, God made me very happy to sit all day and read.

So I'm defined by my incapacities as well as my capacities. When Harry's came out they said, "You're the only type of person we can't help." He tested well in everything. He was good in his writing skills, he was good in his mechanical skills, and he was good in his mathematical skills. And they said that the only other person that they tested that was higher than him in scores was an alcoholic dishwasher.

"A person like you," they said, "who is good in everything, will never be satisfied. There is nothing in life you can do that will ever satisfy you because there's nothing that uses all your powers."

In his case they said, "The only choice you have is to become Thomas Jefferson or an alcoholic dishwasher. You have to somehow find a career where you do a lot of things." Stevie was a better musician, Tommy was a better athlete and I was smarter, so therefore, in effect, he was competing with each of us. And each of us was better in one area that he cared about. But the truth is that Harry was a very, very high quality human being who had a wide range of skills and abilities.

BA: He could have been anything he wanted to be: that was the problem. So that's why he lucked out when he fell into being a star. And then he could do different things.
But the reason he was never exactly settled in his life and the reason he never would have been settled or really happy was that no life he could have led would have satisfied all his skills, so therefore he was always going to be changing.
So if he had not died he would be doing twenty different things now. That's one of the reasons he had that endless energy, which is one of his most profound characteristics.

PF: What sort of literature did he like to read? Can you think of any authors he liked?

JC: I don't think he read many novels.

BA: Oh, he read novels. He read a lot of literature.

PF: What about poetry?

BA: I don't know, but he wrote a lot of poetry.

JC: That's an interesting question. What did Harry read? His reading had less in common with my reading than any of my other brothers. I know he liked the Becker books about denial of death.

BA: I gave him that. He was always reading stuff on planes. He read a lot of stuff you gave him too, Jim. He was reading Gary Wills at that point. He read so much because he traveled a lot.

JC: He would sleep sometimes, but basically he was the type who went 18 or 19 hours a day.

BA: The truth is he slept on airplanes a lot because he wasn't sleeping other places.

PF: Can you imagine what his dreams were like?

BA: Some of the stuff that he dreamed about I'm sure was in his songs.

JC: Well, if you listen to, "a wild man wizard hiding in me illuminating my mind" (*laughs*). Let's face it, my whole family is on the border of schizophrenia. Several people have fallen over that border and I think Harry was pretty close to that border.

BA: The operative thing with Harry, the last major conversation I had with Harry... I always knew when Harry was in trouble.

Jim and I both would know because he would avoid us. He would tend to avoid us when he was in trouble, when he was getting sort of in some place that wasn't good. So one day I corralled him. And I said to him, "What the hell is happening here?" And he said, "You know, I had this experience when I was a teenager and when I started college." He said it was for years. "I was depressed." The worst six months of his life was when he came back from Cornell. It was around 1964 or '65. He was sort of hanging around, but he wasn't doing anything.

PF: He actually stayed in the house a lot, didn't he?

BA: Yeah, and even after when Sandy got to know him, it took a while, but she really helped him come out of his depression. That's one of the reasons that they had a very strong kind of thing going for a very long time because she really helped him to get out of the depression.

   He said to me, "I will never forget what that was like. I never want to be there again." So he said to me, and this was the thing that helped me understand him more than anything else, he said to me, "So, every time that I feel any of that coming up on me, I just run faster. That's what I've been doing. I've been running faster to get away from it."

JC: The period that he becomes a star...if you look at the incredible negotiations. By sheer willpower, he lifted himself. He was calling everybody and doing all that stuff for himself. He went through this incredible emotional mud.

   When, like everyone else in the world would say, "Holy shit," Harry does this. I mean he could live in a sort of chaos and somehow master it.

BA: It was exciting to him.

JC: No matter what disaster hit him, three days later he's

bouncing up again. He goes through this huge crisis and by God he's out there again. Most of us try to organize our lives in some way to avoid crisis and tension and high-pressure situations—Harry set it up so it happened.

BA: (*laughing*) Exactly.

JC: And Harry thrived on it.

BA: That's one reason why Harry had such an effect on people. Because people wouldn't know all of the stuff that we're talking about here. What they would catch would be the energy. They would catch the dazzlement.

JC: And also the magic.

BA: Yes, and the magic.

PF: What about the human side of him?

JC: He was a very human person. They saw someone who told them that you didn't have to be a saint, but you could still be a good person.

PF: But they couldn't see all the dimensions of him?

BA: Of course not. You can't see it on the stage. But what they saw was a lot more dimensions than anyone else that stood on those stages.

James Chapin gets called out of the room to take a phone call as I continue talking with Bill Ayres.

PF: What happened once he became famous and was also involved in WHYHunger?

BA: He didn't have to give that up. What he realized was that he wanted to be a superstar, more than anything. He wrote a song about this—"The Star Tripper." That was the story about what happened after we started doing all the stuff together. He came to recognize that there was more to life than fame.

I got into another level of relationship with him because there were some marital problems. So I kind of helped him out in that area. Part of what I was trying to say was: "Look, you got something here that is very valuable. Don't blow it. And don't be moving so fast that you are going to miss these little kids." So we talked about what is now called quality time.

In those days, people weren't using that term so much. We spent a lot of time together. He came to see that even if he had all that stuff, it didn't mean shit if he lost what was most important to him.

He could walk into any concert hall or theater in America and turn on a few thousand people, or eight or ten thousand people, maybe. But after you do that for a while, what do you do then? What's the next step?

I was reading something just this morning where this guy said, "What is unconditional love? What's real love in the human experience?" It's really a sense of being home because home is where they accept you for who you are.

You don't have to perform. Harry wanted to have that experience because he didn't have it growing up. So he tried to create it for his kids. He tried to make sure that nobody was going to get beat up; nobody was going to get abused.

PF: Didn't he drive all the way from places like Buffalo to get home in the morning so that he would be with his kids when they woke up?

BA: Absolutely. The kids would go to bed at night and he would be gone and he would get in at three, four, five, six o'clock in the morning and he would be cooking breakfast for them when they woke up.

We always thought that he would die on one of these sort of Jim Croce-type of airplane deals. If the airlines couldn't take him someplace, and he wanted to get home for a soccer game, he would find some little guy who had a plane someplace and he would say, can you take me to, wherever, and the guy would say, "Yeah." And he'd pay the guy and get on the little plane with him, and he'd go. He did that all the time.

PF: Why do you think that a lot of music critics were so rough on Harry Chapin?

BA: I think it's partially because he dealt with the stuff of life in such a right-out-there way. His songs were evocative. And they touch people very deeply. Harry was dealing with the real stuff of life. And I don't think those guys got it.

John Wallace said something beautiful about Harry. John said, "Harry was never mean-spirited." The thing I said to you before. He said, "Harry was very forgiving and he never tried to hurt people. He never tried to put people down. He always tried to make people more than they were."

Now when you think about that, Harry made people more. He felt that if the people around him were more he would be too. So he didn't need to put you down for him to be more. He needed to call forth your talent, your creativity, and then he would be more.

PF: Was he involved in any particular religion in any way?

BA: No. He had grown up as an Episcopalian. Now that's an interesting story. We had three lengthy discussions about God that I remember, several other little snippets. The first one he basically said, knowing I was a priest, he said, "I'm an agnostic. I come from a long history of agnostics and atheists. I'm not an atheist. I don't say definitely that there is no God. I just don't know. It would be nice if it's there, but I'm not counting on it."

And then somewhere in the middle of our relationship he started asking a lot of questions because he saw as we got into this that some of the best people he met that were dealing with hunger were church people. And that shocked him. (*soft laugh*) He didn't think that would happen. And he said, "I believe in the believers." So there was definitely an openness that developed.

PF: Do you think that with his music the good stuff was yet to come?

BA: Yeah, I think so. Sure. But I think that one of Harry's problems, in terms of albums, I think he made some bad judgments about some of the songs that he put on the albums, and it weakened them. They were songs that he believed in so much that he just wanted to get them out there and put them on record. Then he never sang them.

I used to say to him, "You know if you're not singing something, why the hell put it on the record?" He'd say, "Well, it's a good song." So each record had some real gems on it, but some other things that were not gems. The *Greatest Stories Live* album is really the best album he ever did because for one thing, it's him live.

Harry was one of the greatest live performers in the history of the music world. But Harry was not a great recording artist. Harry got bored. Harry would be in a recording studio and he'd be bored to death. He'd be on the phones making phone calls about hunger, about this and that, and someone would say, "Harry, it's your turn to do a vocal," and he'd run in, do the damn vocal and he'd get back on the phone again.

I said to him one time just before he died, I said to him, he was doing his last album, I said, "Harry why don't we get about a hundred people, fifty people, twenty people, I don't care. We'll bring them in the studio and let's let them sit there and be an audience for you. You do best when you have a live audience." And he said, "Yeah, I've thought about that, but I'm not going to do that. It's too fragmented. They wouldn't enjoy it."

He just never got comfortable in a studio as far as I could tell, but boy, you put him out on that stage and the stage was his living room. He wrote an album called *Living Room Suite* and the basic idea there was that whatever size auditorium he was in, it would become an extension of his living room. So you were being invited into an intimate experience. He had magic with an audience. There are only a few people that I've known who do that. Bruce Springsteen could do it.

PF: What singers did Harry Chapin influence?

BA: I think he influenced Billy Joel. Billy Joel said he did.

PF: Was he influenced in any way by Don McLean?

BA: Harry thought that one of the best songs that were ever written was "Starry Starry Night." He absolutely loved that song. And he used to tell McLean that. He'd say, "I wished that I'd written that song. And I wouldn't say that about too many songs."

PF: Was Harry Chapin a lonely man?

BA: (Pause) Probably. But then again, I think that is part of the human condition. I think that there is something in each of us that is alone and that there is also in each of us something that is radically communal. We have a great desire to be bonded. And Harry had that desire too. And yet the demons moved him so fast that there wasn't a lot of time for bonding. And that's why if you wanted to be Harry Chapin's friend you really had to work at it. (*laughs softly*)

PF: Why?

BA: Because he would run away. Or he would be moving too fast. First of all, he had to slow down. I said to him one time,

"Harry, most people operate on thirty-three and a third, I might operate on forty-five, I think I move faster than most people." (*At this point Bill raised the volume and speed of his voice.*) You operate on seventy-eight! Nobody can go that fast. It sounds like a bunch of chipmunks. He moved so fast it was just very hard for him to slow down to have a relationship with anyone.

He was always moving, going on to something else. It was very hard to get Harry to be present with you over a long period of time. We did it, though. It happened. James did it as his brother. His wife Sandy did it. Very few people did that. And that was hard for him to do. It was very hard because it was exposing.

Point Lookout, NY

WHAT MADE AMERICA FAMOUS

**"We lived in the house that made
America famous. It was a rundown
slum, the shame of all the decent folks
in town. We hippies and some welfare cases,
Crowded families of coal black faces..."**

Point Lookout, Long Island, is a small hamlet that feels different from Long Island's trendy beach towns like East Hampton or Sag Harbor. It's only 11 blocks long, 3 blocks wide, and surrounded by water.

There's no mail delivery to homes—you go down to the post office and pick up your letters and bills. A lot of the residents get around on bicycles. The speed limit is 15 miles an hour. Two famous people used to come and live there in the summer: Marlene Dietrich, and the legendary strong man, Charles Atlas. At least, that's what some of the locals tell you. That's what they're proud of.

Point Lookout is probably one of the last towns left in America where you can stop someone walking down Main Street on a Sunday afternoon and they will know the name of the person you're looking for. For about eight or nine years, starting in the mid '60s, Harry Chapin and his wife Sandy lived there. She came first, years earlier, trying to escape the harshness of the city and a marriage to the son of the Brooklyn Borough President that wasn't working.

Harry met Sandy back in Brooklyn Heights, where he gave her guitar lessons. He later wrote a song about it that captured a turning point in Sandy's life, "I Wanna Learn a Love Song." And she did.

Harry Chapin watched Point Lookout with his writer's eyes, and many years later summed it all up in an epic of a song called, "What Made America Famous." The song had so much power that it was produced as a Broadway play. *The Night That Made America Famous* would run on Broadway for 75 performances. Along with Harry, his brothers Tom and Steve performed in the cast and brought as much talent to the production as he did.

But the people in Point Lookout were not happy with this play about their town. The play and song caught all the small-town misery and drama of Sherwood Anderson's Winesburg, Ohio. It told a story about a welfare house filled with poor, mostly black, people and a fire that started there on Christmas night, and it insinuated that the local fire department took their time getting to it as the building burned down, though the firehouse was just down the block.

I drove to Point Lookout one early spring afternoon to seek the ghost of Harry Chapin, whose memory lives on in the streets and bars of the town he made so famous in this controversial song. The beach at the end of Harry's former block is probably one of the most beautiful beaches on Long Island. As in Montauk, rows of sand bluffs fringe an amazing view of the Atlantic Ocean. In the first days of April, Point Lookout is a slow, lazy shore town. Streets are empty and silent. People are just starting to awaken from the cold winter. I walk past Harry's old house at 69 Cedarhurst Avenue. Just up the block, on the corner of Lido Boulevard, the fire immortalized in his song had raged.

A few bikers pedal by me. They all seem to ride old-fashioned two-wheelers, bright red or blue, with balloon tires and no extra speed gears. Here and there, you see one of them parked outside one of the local stores. They are not locked up.

On Lido Boulevard I approach the Point Lookout Realty Office—the first place you notice when you're coming into this town, and the last place you see when you're leaving. Paul Gomez and his mother Rosemary run it. Rosemary befriended Sandy Chapin at an uncertain time in her life, when she really needed someone to talk to.

When you listen to Paul talk about his friend Harry Chapin, he brings you back with him to a Point Lookout of the '60s, where Harry regularly walked the streets: "We played basketball all the time together at the Bishop Malloy recreation center. You would always see him playing. He loved exercise. Sometimes he would even shoot hoops by himself."

Paul talks about how he would bring songs that he wrote to Harry Chapin, and ask him for advice. "Harry would rate each line. That was the way he did it. He scribbled. I have a whole bunch of the manuscripts that he worked on. I still have them here. And he would, like, cross out every single line. He would laugh and say, 'But I like the title of the song.'

"He rated each different line, A, B, C or D. 'That's an A line,' he would say. 'You got to keep it.' And, 'I love that title. That's an A title.'" Harry Chapin became a mentor for Paul, and eventually the two of them became as close as brothers. Paul was a teenager when they met, and Harry was 29.

"He always said, 'The last line should be the best. The last line should always be the best. Has to be the A-plus line,' he would say."

Paul sings the last line from "Taxi" for me: "'I go flying so high when I'm stoned.' That's a great line."

He remembers how Harry got involved in trying to help the young people in Point Lookout.

"He started a little coffee house in the old firehouse. It says 'Ye Old Firehouse' on the front of it now. Sandy said to him one day, 'Harry, there's too many kids hanging around on the streets in this town. They have nothing to do. They're just sitting around smoking cigarettes, drinking beer, getting in trouble. Why don't you start a little coffee house for the kids, so they could come in and do something artsy?' This must have been about in the late '60s.

"But there was a backlash against him. Harry just had too much energy for most people in this town. Someone said that he was too rich for the town." Paul explains that he doesn't mean rich as in money. "Big fish, little pond. Rich internally, in spirit. He lived at 69 Cedarhurst Avenue. It's right around the corner from here. It was the original Harry Chapin house, but they just renovated it. They put some new siding on it."

"You would think that somebody would have put a plaque on his old house by now," I say to him. "He was one of America's greatest songwriters, one of America's greatest performers. But except for the few people who remember him, it's as if he never existed down here."

Paul agrees. "You know, this town doesn't have a vision for greatness; they don't have appreciation for greatness. They are all 'too great' themselves. You know? There is something about the people in this town. They just don't appreciate someone like Harry Chapin. He was truly alive. He truly wanted to do things."

"It's a typical day and Harry Chapin is walking down the main street. What are the local folks saying?" I ask him.

"'There goes Harry. Oh, there goes Harry.'"

"So he stood out."

"He definitely stood out. We used to play basketball all the time. You know, you have your own small town rules, playing two on two, three on three. Harry, it was funny; it was an eye-opener for everyone because he started his own rules. When the ball exchanged hands, exchanged teams, you used to go behind the foul line. You have to get the ball behind and your whole body behind; he would just get his foot behind and take a shot. I'll never forget that. We used to call it 'Harry rules.'"

"What was the reaction by the town folks when he put together that play, and they find out that their small town is up on the lights on Broadway?"

"That was quite upsetting. There are some real stories that the world should know about this town. No wonder Harry took it upon himself to try to incorporate that into a Broadway play, *The Night That Made America Famous*. There was a little tenement house here. Now it's a park where all the kids smoke drugs. They should go bless that place, somehow, and put some holy water around it, you know? It's inherited a bad aura and the families who live around it hate it.

"As the story goes, the town fire department, which is just around the corner, shows up there for a fire one night, and they have Christmas music coming from the truck's cab. This is around the holidays. And the house burns down to the ground.

"A lot of people thought that it was intentional. But I guess you really couldn't prove it. I wasn't there, but I heard the stories about the guys playing Christmas music while it's burning down.

"A lot of people didn't like Harry Chapin. A lot of them butted heads with him. They were always talking about Harry. But I don't think that it affected him. He just thought that this place was too small and he had to get out."

"Why did they dislike him so much?"

"Like I said, he just had too much energy for them. He was an idealist. People don't like that kind of energy in small towns. When the song was released, people were outraged. They thought they were singled out, like the plumber, the electrician. What is he implying here? That's the whole question."

Paul starts to remember the good times he had with Harry in Point Lookout. "My sister used to babysit for Sandy's children. So before he married Sandy I knew him. I knew them when he was jobless. He was doing three, four, five things at the same time. He used to invite our family over on a music night in the '60s all the time. Come on over, he would say. We're playing music. I played piano.

"This is down here in Point Lookout before he ever made it. The family used to always have a music night. I was a young teenager, about fourteen or fifteen years old. This is about '66 or '67. Harry and Sandy used to save everything. 'Save that little pasta. Save everything you can.' They gave my sister instructions, 'Everything you can save, save.'"

"They were down on their luck then?"

"They were down. Sandy came out for a summer rental with the three little ones: Jono, Jason, and Jamie. I think my mother really knew that Sandy never wanted to go back to Brooklyn. My mom made it comfortable for her to stay in that house. I don't know if it was one that we owned, or one that was on the market. But she made it comfortable to stay there and she didn't have to go back."

"When you were around him in Point Lookout, did you say to yourself, this guy is going to rocket up there someday? He's going to be a star?"

"He had a type-A personality. He wanted to be the best. I saw it back then. He was a true-to-form person and that's why in this town they wanted to see him leave, because he exposed the truth about things."

"How long did Sandy and he live in Point Lookout?"

"I think it's like '64, or '65 to maybe seven or eight years, nine years [later]. I met him through my family. We know Sandy, and then all of a sudden Harry shows up. We met him through Sandy. He's just a guy from Brooklyn, a boyfriend. And then Harry comes out and lives with them.

"Not too long after that, I'll never forget this day, I see Sandy in a little Volkswagen right here at this gas station." He points out the window of his office. "I'm pulling around the corner; I see her get out of the Volkswagen in her wedding gown. She's going to get married to Harry."

"On the last day of his life, weren't you one of the people waiting at a party for him that day in Oyster Bay? Weren't you supposed to drive him that day?"

"Sandy liked to have someone drive him around because he was a crazy driver. I used to drive him a lot. Right up until when he died, I was driving him. I must have been about 29 when he died. He needed a driver because he was always tired after the concerts. He was a crazy driver so Sandy felt better that I drive."

Paul thinks back to the day Harry Chapin died: July 16, 1981. He talks about how he was supposed to drive him into New York for some business, and then drive him back to a pre-concert party at his manager Don Ruthig's house. That was Harry Chapin's last concert.

"I was supposed to drive him to New York that morning, and then wait for him in the car. I can't remember what it was for." (Harry was actually driving in for a meeting with brother/manager Jeb Hart and Harry's booking agent Shelly Schultz. It was a meeting that Harry had blown off the day before: a meeting to read Harry the riot act about how many benefits he was doing, how that was hurting his career, how there was a better, more logical way to do both—make more money for WHYHunger and help his "career.")

"Then I was supposed to drive him to a party at Don Ruthig's place. I think it was in Oyster Bay Cove. It had a big pool. It was for the Eisenhower Park Concert. His whole family was there. The band was there. It was a pre-concert party in the afternoon. Everybody was there.

"Harry called me that morning or Sandy called me that morning, or I called them, and Harry said 'Paul, don't come over. I'm going to go in early.' That was the word."

"Harry told you this?"

"Sandy wanted me to come in and drive him. It was the day he died. She wanted me to pick him up in Huntington, drive him into to New York and come back out. We had picked out a time I was going to pick him up. I think it was nine o'clock.

"I called and she said that he had already gone, or that he's going to go earlier. He's going to get on the road earlier so that he can get back early for the party. Everybody was there. It was a festive thing, a celebration of the concert. All of his close friends were there. His whole band was there. His family was there. His wife was there. There must have been at least 50 or 60 people.

"I'll never forget that as we were waiting for him to arrive, I was standing next to Don Ruthig because he was the guy who would always give you the scoop. He was his personal manager and he was on top of everything. We're talking and we're saying, 'Well Harry must be late, the meeting must have been late in New York.'

"So then we heard from some of the people coming to the party that they got stuck in traffic. 'There was a terrible accident and we got stuck in traffic.' Then someone called in saying, 'We're stuck in traffic.' So we thought that Harry is stuck in the same traffic.

"Then an hour goes by and we're thinking, *but why didn't Harry call? He usually calls ahead. He stops at a gas station and he calls.* There were no cell phones then. We don't hear from him and all of a sudden, everyone is concerned.

"You could hear the mumble. All of a sudden, we get a call from somebody passing through that it was a Volkswagen Rabbit and that it was charred, burnt. Some big truck rammed it in the back. 'I passed it,' someone says. 'It was a Volkswagen Rabbit.'

"Then you could see everybody like—God almighty. I looked at Sandy and she was white as a ghost. And then the call finally came in. Don was almost losing it. He started screaming, yelling, wailing. I think it was Big John Wallace who went over to him and said 'Don, don't do this to yourself. Don't do this.'

"We were all just shocked. We just walked around in silence. I came home to Point Lookout and I started crying. I didn't cry until I got home. I pulled into my driveway and I just cried. I'll never forget that night."

"Harry was a big brother to me. We played basketball together; we listened to music together. That's before he ever made it. He was always on the run. When I knew him earlier, he always said, 'Dream big dreams, Paul. Go after your big dreams.'

"But he was a man of conflicts. Toward the end of his life,

he said to me, 'Paul, maybe it's better that we don't reach our dreams, because you wonder if we can handle it. It could be the demon that we can't live up to.'

"He was constantly trying to live up to that stardom. He wanted to be a star, but then he wanted to be a family man. This is tough. But he did it."

STAR TRIPPER

"But the star tripper's coming back home now. It's a crazy blind man's journey he's been on.

The star tripper's lost and all alone now. And it's your face he'd like to look upon. Yes, he's praying that you won't be long gone..."

Drinking With People Who Live In a Song

"He was so outgoing and he believed that everybody loved him, and therefore, everybody did. Of course, when he got older life got a little more complicated, but he started that way. He was the sweetest child in the world."

—Harry's mom, Elspeth Hart
(From my interview in her Brooklyn home)

After leaving Paul Gomez, I decide to walk around Point Lookout to see if I might get more sense of what this town is about. I walk down to the small public park on Lido Boulevard where the infamous house from "What Made America Famous" once stood before it burnt to the ground. What's there now are four benches, a few small pine trees. Not much space, maybe 30 feet by 30 feet. This park is right up the corner from Harry's former block, about six houses up from where he lived.

I stroll for a while down Lido Boulevard, past the building where Harry Chapin started a coffee house for the local kids to keep them out of trouble. Some of them are still around I'm told, older now and hanging out in the local bar on Lido Boulevard, The Bay House Lounge.

I walk through the entire town, which does not take long. Cutting down a side street, I get lost in the silence of the morning. There is parking up on Lido Boulevard, but not on these side streets. So if you're an outsider who doesn't live here you are going to have a hard time coming to Point Lookout to hang around.

It feels like a small New England fishing village. I walk past a few clam bar restaurants on Bayside Drive, some fishing stations, a marina from where the charter fishing boats leave. I pass by Scotty's Fishing Station, but it's still closed for winter during the week.

I stop at Teddy's Fishing Station, which is just up the block from it. A young man is busy scraping down a large wooden fishing boat, getting it ready for the rental season. He stops when he sees me and we talk about fishing. "Man, the flounder fishing is so bad they ought to close it down for a couple of years. Forget about the fluke fishing. There just ain't any flounder around anymore," he says. I nod my head in agreement with him and move on.

Later as I walk in the front door of The Bay House Lounge, I can't help but feel like an outsider. *It's not going to be easy walking out of here with an interview*, I think as I look at the hard face of the barmaid staring at me.

"No tap beer," she tells me. "Bottles only." I order a bottle of Budweiser, and look around as I get settled down. After a while, I order another beer and I ask the barmaid about Harry Chapin living here. I tell her I'm a writer. She really doesn't say much about him, yet doesn't seem too upset by the mention of his name.

I stare straight ahead at my reflection in the mirror as I drink the beer. The young lady next to me turns. "You're a writer?" she asks.

I answer with a short "Yeah."

"What are you writing?"

I tell her that I'm writing about Harry Chapin, and that I just spoke with Paul Gomez from Point Realty about him.

"Me and Paul Gomez went to Catholic school together," she says.

I ask her if she remembers the coffee house that Harry Chapin started.

"Yeah, I remember it, and I remember how the guys used to play half-court basketball with Harry Chapin in the Bishop Molloy recreation hall on Parkside Drive. On the other half was us kids playing volleyball." And she remembers seeing Harry Chapin playing in those half-court games. He was just starting to become famous. I think that's where he got the street name "16 Parkside Lane" in his song "Taxi."

"Once, he invited a bunch of us to go to the Bitter End in the Village in Manhattan when he played there. He got us in for nothing. You know who he was playing second fiddle to? Cheech and Chong. I gave Cheech a life-saver." She laughs. The whole bar laughs.

"Are you sure that was a life-saver?" someone yells across the room.

"The coffee house he started was good. There was nowhere to go in this town, nowhere to hang out. If the recreation hall wasn't open, you would be outside and freezing in the winter. So at least we had the coffee house with the jukebox and you could get a soda."

I ask her what she thought about his song about Point Lookout, "What Made America Famous."

"You want me to be blunt about it—the chubby-cheeked firemen and the night that made America famous? That's a load of crap as far as what really happened. Those firemen did the best they could. It was a Christmas tree that started the fire, and if you want to go into the records, you'll find that out. It was not the fault of the firemen at all.

"There was no way that they didn't do their job that night. I stood on the corner by the gas station and witnessed it. I saw a guy go up, and pull the Christmas tree out with the Christmas lights still on it and throw it on the fire escape.

I've retired from the New York City fire department since then, so I kind of know what I'm talking about. But that song does piss people off, because it wasn't true that they didn't do anything just because black people lived there."

"So you guys think that he just made that song up?"

"The point of it, I think, is not true, "she says. "In other words, the song suggests that the firemen purposely did not do their jobs and let the place burn down. I say that's totally not true. Not true. They're volunteer firemen. I mean they could have just not shown up."

Someone a few stools away yells out, "Exactly!"

Time has been stirred up on this spring afternoon in a town that will live forever in a Harry Chapin song. A silence rolls across the room as I leave.

The Real Mr. Tanner

MR. TANNER

**"Mr. Tanner was a cleaner from a town in the Midwest.
And of all the cleaning shops around he'd made his the best.
But he also was a baritone who sang while hanging clothes.
He practiced scales while pressing tails and sang at local shows."**

It's been a long, slow ride on I-95. Ahead of me are lines and lines of rowed up tractor-trailers, shrugging and hissing. I can see them above the curve of the highway. The only distraction for me as traffic crawls along is a CD. I listen to the lyrics of "Mr. Tanner," which I've heard many times before. Only now am I headed up to Connecticut to interview the real Mr. Tanner, a man who will live forever inside these lyrics.

In 1974, "Mr. Tanner" became part of a Chapin album titled *Short Stories*. This beautiful song about not letting failure totally destroy you—about hope—describes an opera singer who dreams of one day leaving his dry cleaning shop in Dayton, Ohio and being recognized for his talent. For years, his friends who have heard him sing have encouraged him to rent a hall in New York and let the world hear his voice.

**"Finally they got to him; he would take the fling...
It took most of his savings but he gladly used them all.
But music was his life, it was not his livelihood,
And it made him feel so happy and it made him feel so good..."**

Harry Chapin got the idea after reading two separate *New York Times* concert reviews of two separate performances that held nothing back in their criticism of a bass-baritone singer named Martin Tubridy, who performed at them both. Each review was about five lines long. Chapin, who never forgot a few of his own hurtful reviews, held onto them until the story of Mr. Tanner started to form into a song in his head, and a profound character was born.

"Mr. Martin Tanner, Baritone, of Dayton, Ohio made his Town Hall debut last night. He came well prepared, but unfortunately his presentation was not up to contemporary professional standards. His voice lacks the range of tonal color necessary to make it consistently interesting. Full-time consideration of another endeavor might be in order."

With just a few short lines a *New York Times* music critic destroyed his dreams.

**"He came home to Dayton and was questioned by his friends.
Then he smiled and just said nothing and he never sang again,
Excepting very late at night when the shop was dark and closed.
He sang softly to himself as he sorted through the clothes."**

Mr. Tanner's story would have ended there if not for Howie Fields, the drummer for the Chapin Family Band, who contacted Martin Tubridy in 2016. It was at the same time that the Chapin Family Band was doing a charity fundraiser in Fairfield, Connecticut. When Howie got Tubridy on the phone he asked him to appear at the fundraiser and sing the part of Mr. Tanner in the song. Would he sing "O Holy Night" along with Big John Wallace, who does it on the CD?

The request for him to go on stage, and to sing part of "Mr. Tanner" in front of a huge audience sounded surreal to Tubridy. In effect, he would be making himself vulnerable to the risk of reliving the Town Hall night of rejection, the night of pain once more. Howie Fields had assured him that the night would go well: "The audience there will be all for you; they'll be all for Harry Chapin." Fields even told him that there was a cult following for the song. Mike Grayeb, a board member at the Harry Chapin Foundation, also helped convince Tubridy to get back on stage. Finally, he agreed. What Howie Fields did not know was that night Big John Wallace wouldn't be able to make it, and Martin Tubridy would be asked to sing the whole part himself—the part of Mr. Tanner.

His performance can be seen on YouTube. So far, there are over 25,000 views of him with the Harry Chapin band. Some viewers commented that they were moved to tears. Another called the performance "surreal." Tubridy received a standing ovation that night and cheers from the crowd.

Neil Steinberg, a writer for the *Chicago Times* somehow heard about the YouTube video with the Chapin band and was moved to write a column about it. In fact, he turned the original *New York Times* review into a rave review for Martin Tubridy. The *Chicago Times* ran the story on their front page on Christmas Eve in 2016.

Once off the highway, it's an easy ride to Mr. Tanner's house. The Tubridys live in a country home in the back, winding roads of Connecticut with carefully piled stone walls that flank either side. As I get closer, I think that meeting him now in person will be like meeting a character that walked out of a quintessential American short story, like a Salinger story. I see him waiting in the doorway as I walk up the driveway. Next to him stands his wife, Marlane.

"Mr. Tanner," I say, smiling as I put my hand forward to greet him. And then I add "Mr. Tubridy," as he smiles back at me.

They invite me to sit at the kitchen table where we will have lunch. Looking out the wide picture window next to it you see a surging stream. Beyond it are rows and rows of tall trees.

Martin Tubridy has been living here for almost thirty years. He's originally from Astoria, Queens.

Talking to him, you quickly get the feeling that he is a spiritual, modest man who lives his life conservatively—not unlike Harry Chapin's character, Mr. Tanner. His website reveals a few facts about him: lists of his favorite music, favorite books, and also his favorite pictures. It's no surprise that many beloved photos are of Ireland, like the Cliffs of Moher. He has roots in Ireland, he says. His family traces their heritage back to a town called Tuam, in County Galway.

Marlane places a quiche pie with broccoli and cheese on the table, and then Martin adds some homemade grain bread and a goat cheese salad he has made. It's followed by hot tea and slices of layer cake. The perfect way to spend an afternoon with "Mr. Tanner," I'm thinking.

"Did you ever hear Mr. Tanner on the radio before you were told that it was you Harry Chapin was writing about? Before you realized that you were Mr. Tanner?" I ask him.

"As you listen to music a lot of times it registers with you, and sometimes it does not. It was only when I became aware of it did it tie in precisely," he says.

"When I first heard 'Mr. Tanner' and then later read the *New York Times* review that inspired him to write it, I wondered how did Harry take something like that, a one-paragraph, four-line review and turn it into an opera? It takes a certain type of creative genius to do that," I say.

"I think he was very much tuned into other people," Marlane says. "And he really listened."

"The amazing thing about 'Mr. Tanner,'" Martin Tubridy says, "is that he followed one review, and I was surprised about that, but the amazing thing is that he searched out and found the other review. There were two reviews, one was at Carnegie Hall, and the other was at Town Hall. And I'm thinking he probably had enough to write on with one of those, and he got the gist of it, of rejection.

"He basically took some of the quotes directly from the reviews. There's got to be a lot of empathy there. He must have looked at that review and there was something that clicked in him that said creatively, I can put something together, but probably also he emphasized with the person who got this review, and how he felt. So that's all amazing."

I wonder how he came up with having Mr. Tanner come from Dayton, Ohio. I ask him.

"Well it's Middle America," he answers. "And I think that's what he was looking for. My guess, anyway. The thing about it all for me, which is surreal, is that there are hundreds of people who are reviewed each year in the *New York Times*, and how it just happened that that review stuck out in his mind. He latched on to that one and a beautiful song was created from it."

It's clear that Martin Tubridy never forgot that night and the *New York Times* review. He still has the original poster from the Town Hall Concert. It shows a young man wearing a dark suit, hair perfectly in place, tie just right as he confidently stares out from the frame. Below his picture are the bold words: "TOWN HALL MARTIN TUBRIDY BASS-BARITONE TUESDAY EVENING AT 8.00 FEBRUARY 15."

He went on to relive, and improve, that night of destiny.

Tubridy describes how he first felt when he heard people speculate that he was Mr. Tanner. "Initially, I felt a lot of resentment that I was being associated with the song. I started to receive phone calls from different parts of the country. One was from Long Island, another from the Boston area. Years later, I started getting emails looking for verification that I was Martin Tubridy, I was Mr. Tanner, and going, 'No, no, no. It's not me.' And total denial because I had no idea I was getting closer to being a part of that."

"Did you think it might become a problem at some point?" I ask him.

"Yeah. I did. I kept saying, 'No, I'm not from Dayton Ohio;

no, I'm not from the Midwest, no this, and no that.' I really thought it was all untrue, and I even asked my sons, how can we get rid of this? How do we disassociate?

"Then Howie Fields sent an email in 2016, and later he telephoned me asking if I would be interested in talking to him about a performance."

"Did he start the phone call by asking if you were the real Mr. Tanner?"

Martin Tubridy smiles as he says, "Well that's what he initially said: 'Are you Martin Tanner?' After all these years I started believing that (the song) was all about me, and finally accepting that it was. But prior to that I had no reason to believe because nobody that knew Harry Chapin was telling me that he had the reviews. It was when someone who was close to Harry Chapin approached the subject that I started to believe, my God this is real."

He talks about the night of the Mr. Tanner performance.
"Harry Chapin had intensely loyal followers. I think anyone who was at that performance that night...I think anyone who goes to these performances has deep...I want to say has a deep love, affiliation, closeness to him. And they see—they see him almost like a Mother Teresa. They see someone that is not just taking, taking, taking, but someone who wants to go and help and give. There was something about Harry Chapin that his whole life was about doing something about hunger.

"And I caught on to all that and that's what Howie Fields was describing. He said the audience there will be all for you; they'll be all for Harry Chapin. My concern obviously was how do I go up there and not screw it up again." (*He laughs*).

"But the people in the audience, the Harry Chapin family, all of them, they were just wonderful," he says.

"You hit on some very interesting things about Harry's audience and the family. There is almost ... uh, spiritual is the wrong word," I say.

"No. That's the right word," he answers. "I didn't want to

say it, but that's the right word, spiritual. You're talking about something above the norm. I mean you can get the norm anywhere. This was something special. These people are special, not only the family, but also the audience.

"I think not only Harry Chapin, but all of the people around him are very much on a different level. When I got to meet them I thought, *They're all givers in one way or another.* They weren't thinking about themselves. I mean at that concert in Fairfield Connecticut, and I'm sure it happened many times in other places they were devoting their own time and energy to a cause. There was also a devotion to Harry Chapin, what they knew about him, how their relationship with him came about. It was beautiful to see that devotion.

"That night there was a pre-concert party, cocktails and stuff, and people were coming up to me giving me incredible hugs. They recognized me from a previous interview I did with Mike Grayeb and Tom Chapin. They recognized me and gave me just incredible hugs and friendliness.

"When Howie Fields first mentioned my doing this I was intrigued. I said to Marlane, 'What do you think?' and she's going, 'I don't know. It may be best to just let it lie. You had the experience several years ago. You don't want to get involved in all this again, 'she said.

"I went to our two sons and they said, 'Dad, don't even think about it. Don't do it. You can go on with your life. You don't need that now.' They didn't want me to get hurt. I could understand it. They just saw that as too real of a possibility. But there was something in me that, I don't know, needed …. I kept on wondering why is this happening?"

"Did you feel that you wanted another shot at it?" I ask him.

"Yeah. I kept wondering why is this happening after so many years, that I'm getting the opportunity to resolve something from long ago. I think that is when I said yes to it. There was more at play here."

When I had entered the house I passed a room filled with

two pianos, a long keyboard and other musical equipment. The room leads into the kitchen area where we are sitting. I point toward it.

"Late at night, when you're alone, do you ever sit in that room and sing like you did at Carnegie Hall?"

"What do you mean, like Mr. Tanner?" And then he softly says, "No."

Later, as I drove back down on I-95 toward New York, I couldn't help but wonder what Harry Chapin would have felt if he had been at that concert the night the real Mr. Tanner sang "O Holy Night."

Bananas In Scranton, PA

Thirty Thousand Pounds of Tragedy

"It was just after dark when the truck started down
the hill that leads into Scranton, Pennsylvania
carrying thirty thousand pounds of bananas..."

"He was a young driver just out on his second job, and he's carrying
the next day's pasty fruits for everyone in this coal-scarred city..."

My conversation about Harry Chapin's life will continue in bar rooms and bus depots, from Scranton, Pennsylvania to Cape Cod, to Gloucester, Massachusetts, and all across New York State to as far north as Watertown, and out to the middle west of Detroit and Flint, Michigan.

Along the way, I will learn a lot about small-town America and the people who live in the names on our maps. I will learn how critically such spots factor into the measurement of the American Dream.

Scranton, Pennsylvania was one of them, just off of Route 80—the town that Harry Chapin wrote about in his song, "30,000 Pounds of Bananas," an account of a fatal trucking accident.

For years, I vacationed on a lake in Pennsylvania located about a mile from Route 307, the road where the trailer in Harry's song crashed, in real life. Before the interstate came to this area of Pennsylvania, Route 307 was the main route into downtown Scranton. In winter it could become a roller coaster of icy hell.

I often drove on it not knowing its history, not knowing about the trailer crash that killed a local driver on a gray March day in 1965. The Vietnam War was starting to pull more and more young men out of hardscrabble towns like this, and here was more sorrow to bear.

As you drive on it now you can still see the old rusted motel signs of another era on the roadside. For example, a bar and restaurant called The Old Brook Inn that dates back to World War II, remains. It was once a roadhouse where sailors and soldiers from New York City would go to on leave.

Up until a few years ago, they still had the old, shiny oak dance floor in the restaurant area where soldiers would dance with some of the local women who would come up from nearby Scranton. Right next to it is a small, dark bar and a staircase that leads up to private rooms where you could take someone you picked up on the dance floor.

Some years ago, after talking to one of the owners of The Old Brook who lived in the area for a long time, I learned that the banana trailer crash happened just a short driving distance from the bar. Later, after doing research and tracking down newspaper accounts of it in the Scranton library, I realized right away how a tragic event like that would live on in the memories of the people of this small mountain town. The funeral for the driver was held not far from where the accident happened. And all day and into the night the townspeople came to mourn.

Harry wrote in his song that he heard about the trailer crash from a man on a bus going through Scranton, who captured many details about the actual day. In the song, this man on the bus put a humorous twist on it. Talking to some folks up here, I found out it's a tragedy that will be a dark part of their history forever—one they do not joke about.

I ride down to the end of Route 307 to where it turns into Moosic Street, and stand on the spot where the banana trailer finally tipped over. In my hand, I have a black-and-white newspaper picture of the banana trailer and a young man named Eugene P. Sesky, who was driving that day. Looking down at it, I see how the body of the long trailer was pitched over on its side, the entire cab ripped off and thrown, with Eugene P. Sesky still riding the running board toward the house, a few feet away from where I stand.

I ask a vendor at a fruit and vegetable roadside stand if he ever heard the story of the banana trailer that lost its brakes over on nearby Route 307. And when he answers, the look in his eyes and what he was about to tell me, sounds like a Harry Chapin song inside another Harry Chapin song. The odds of my actually meeting him were pretty slim.

"You just raised the hairs on the back of my neck with that question," Bob Ciesielski replies. "My cousin Eugene was driving that trailer." And then he tells his story.

"When I got married and decided what I wanted to do for a living, I chose driving a tractor trailer. I drove for more than 30 years. My mom was always against it," he says, "because of the accident that killed Cousin Eugene. But I just said to her, it could happen to anybody, Mom, and I was just very fortunate that all those years I drove I was accident-free.

"Geanie was my second cousin," he says as he talks about the man in the Harry Chapin song who, in real life, was actually hauling a load of bananas, 15 tons of them, from the docks of Newark, New Jersey to the warehouse of the Atlantic and Pacific store in downtown Scranton.

Ciesielski remembers that he was about 12 years old when it happened back in '65, and how he heard about it from relatives talking.

"Years ago the families all met at my grandmother's home, the old homestead down in Scranton every Sunday. Every Sunday you would have maybe fifteen, twenty people there—aunts, uncles, cousins, anybody that you could think of that was in our family. It's not like today.

"And you would hear them talking and some of the talk you weren't supposed to be around. And I do know that my uncle Butch and my aunt Laura, after this happened, it devastated the both of them.

"The truck hit a house, telephone poles, cars, because it was out of control by that time. It was maybe going, 90, a 100 miles an hour. Once the weight took over, that's it. There was no stopping it.

"You'll still hear people talking about it. As a matter of fact, there's a gentleman who doesn't live too far from me. I don't remember his name. He's trying now to raise funding for some type of memorial.

"There used to be at Moosic Street and Harrison Avenue a little statue in the middle of the road, and a lot of the little children used to play in that area. His own son, Geanie, was one of them. Something happened to either the clutch or something, and he couldn't get it back into gear. He rode the trailer down until eventually it tipped over."

He talks about when he first heard "30,000 Pounds of Bananas."

"I remember hearing it on the radio. It was upsetting for the older people here. As a matter of fact, his son Geanie at one point in his life followed Harry Chapin to different concerts so that he could talk to him and ask him if he could stop playing the song because it would just bring up old memories to the family.

"My cousin Eugene was a very hard-working man for his family. All he was doing was trying to provide a living for them." He paused for a moment. "That was it."

Ever since meeting Eugene Sesky's cousin, I think differently about the song "30,000 Pounds of Bananas." Once you put a face on the tragedy of that day, the humor starts to fade a bit. Even Harry started to realize that. He originally wrote it as a poem about the senselessness of the Vietnam War and the mounting, daily body count, and how the grim numbers coming in each day were getting lost in the coldness and ennui of endless rows of government statistics. He felt that America was missing what he called "the human story behind" the numbers.

As he traveled around America with "30,000 Pounds of Bananas," playing everything from small town gymnasiums to packed city concert halls, the song went through numerous performances and changes as it evolved into what it eventually became: a novelty song whose deeper meaning was difficult to understand.

In a BBC radio interview in 1977, Harry Chapin described how, after hearing that the Sesky family was upset with the song, he made a special trip to Scranton to meet with them, and to tell them he meant no disrespect. "All of a sudden my whole vision of this song radically changed," he told BBC interviewer Noel Edmonds. After that meeting with the Sesky family, he agreed to never play "30,000 Pounds of Bananas" in Scranton, Pennsylvania again.

Like Bob Ciesielski, the few people who are still around to remember what happened in 1965 on that cold March day in that small, working-class section of Scranton, describe Eugene Sesky as a hero. He sacrificed his own life by riding on the running board of the trailer and steering it for six, steep blocks as he blew the air horn to warn people to get out of the way. You can't even imagine what he was thinking that day as he hung onto the side of his trailer, the wind whipping at his face. His son, Eugene Sesky Jr., would go on to become a trailer driver himself. And he kept the watch that his father was wearing on that final day, the time on it frozen at the time of the crash.

That story song is another example of Harry Chapin's amazing talent for writing about true events that only he seemed to notice, and turning them into lyrics that capture a local American tragedy forever.

On the Road with Harry

The Chapin Foundation Office in Huntington, Long Island gave me access to a large manuscript of a novel Harry wrote but never published called *Candor*. It was based on his song "The Mayor of Candor Lied." While reading the manuscript, I found a long account of how he got the idea to write the song, how he gets many song ideas (he mentions his feelings about all the times he's been on Greyhound busses), how he sees things differently from non-writers. Maybe more than that, it was a lonely portrayal of Harry Chapin on the road late at night, heading home after playing a small town college basketball gym in upstate New York:

New York Route 17. In the old days I had no illusions about time. I knew it was going to be a long trip on that Greyhound bus from the Port Authority. It usually started at midnight. The dregs of the Big Apple gathered there for a monoxide merch (sic) killing. You never dressed up to take the Greyhound cause even if it was clean it smelled as if you were getting dirty.

Back then as we drove into the Lincoln Tunnel I knew I was just beginning what was going to be a vibrating, smelly, aching, sleepless night. Out through New Jersey into the corner of Pennsylvania. Rest stop in Scranton, that magical coal town, slag heaps almost as tall as the surrounding hills. Then back up to into New York State into Binghamton. Time to gird your loins for the final push to Ithaca.

Back then I went to Ithaca to matriculate. If only it had been as sexy as it sounds. In all honesty, my two stints at Cornell were dotted with enough interludes and incidents to give those years a not so entirely undeserved romantic overtone.

Tonight I'm going to be late. Why am I always late? At least it's neighboring Ithaca College and not Cornell. Been on time for all gour (sic) concerts at the old Alma Mater. And I don't need to wonder why. Your ego's on line brother, when you return to headline a concert at the college that busted you out twice a decade before. You want to be early and wander around the scene of former debacles before your imagined "Look who's come back" triumph.

Put on the radio again. Back into auto-pilot in this compact Rent-A-bomb. Can't get a decent music station that'll hold for more than a mile or two yo-yoing up and down the Poconos. Guess it's gotta be good old CBS "All News 88." Might as well hear what the world is doing to us this February of '76.

As I pull through Binghamton at 7 pm looking for the turnoff that'll stagger up to Ithaca they are talking about Elizabeth Ray, the secretary who gives her all but unfortunately can't type for her boss, the Chairman of the Ways and Means Committee. (In 1976 Elizabeth Ray was involved in a sex scandal with Rep Wayne Hays (D-Ohio)) Just the kind of thing to get one feeling patriotic for the bicentennial year. "Oh say can You See."

Twenty miles or so outside of Owego CBS dwindles into jumbled static. I turn off the radio. The road straightens out for a while and I can see up ahead of me, maybe a quarter of a mile, that there is a stoplight. My now idle brain directs me to glance around. I'm in the middle of nowhere, why the light? What could call for such a caution, maybe a crossroad or a railroad track? I'm closer now. I see that there is above and beside it a single streetlight. I have to slow as the stoplight goes amber, then red. I wouldn't have noticed the sign if I hadn't been stopped by the red light. And I wouldn't have been able to read the small sign that was already beside the beam of my headlights if it had not been for the wider glow of the streetlight. A perfectly planned synchronous trio.

Maybe that was why they were there. The sign said "Candor"—pop. 617." I immediately said out loud to the sign and its two accompanying lights, "I bet the Mayor of Candor lies."

How do you explain resonances you hear? They ring, they stick, they send off ripples. This sudden, silly little line found a home in my brain. It had happened before. I had learned to recognize, even welcome the symptoms. I would go with these signs. I had long since learned that the difference between writers and non-writers was not the brilliance of their ideas or the quality of the observatory powers. The difference was in the respect with which they treated the products of their brains.

Non-writers threw them off with only slight regret as they receded. Writers, on the contrary, are hoarders, they milk whatever they see, whatever happened to them. So, I, as a matter of habit and in response to the perhaps never-to-be known causes of such stimuli, started circling the phrase as the light went green and I resumed my drive. I started circling it in the sense that you would walk around either an ancient artifact dug up from the graveyard of your memory or a fresh, smoking meteor rudely arrived into your consciousness after its long journey from oblivion.

And then, after this first cautious perusal, intrigued and made braver by what you see, you start prodding, pushing, turning the substance of the line, the incident, the idea to see if it still moves or sets off sparks. I guess what I really do is look for signs of life.

Suddenly the process stopped. Around a bend in the road I'd come upon the harshness of the spinning flashers of two cop cars pulled over to the side of the road. So I slowed the car once again, this time drawn by that subconscious macabre magnet that seems drawn to the possibilities of someone else's disaster, be it a mere traffic ticket or the more serious aspect of a tragic accident.

With a surge of guilt I saw that it was the latter. A car had swerved off the road violently, directly into a tree. The scene had a heightened bizarre theatricality stirred by the strobe effects of the slowly whirling lights.

In addition, the stage was pinpointed by the two hood spotlights of the police cars. Three policemen were working to pull two victims free from the bloodied, twisted wreckage of metal and glass. A fourth cop, standing with a flashlight on the road, emphatically waves me past the brutality of the scene. I obeyed, shaken as always by the specter of the abrupt finality of life.

(In his notes he talks about the after concert trip back down, heading home.)

It had been a good one. Not great, but good. I hate those gyms anyway. Their acoustics are built to make a lackluster crowd of 500 sound like 20,000 jammed into the Garden going bananas. Gyms aren't built to encompass a decent sound system and 3000 listeners. That plus a "visiting team "dressing room and it did not add up to an esthetic experience. Fifteen minutes late in that setup is no problem.

Four hours if I push it a little. Don't push it too much. Accidents, trees, red flashing lights, waiting for singers too. Got to get some coffee on the way down. Either in Binghamton or in one of the greasy spoons off route 17. Light up a cigar and settle in for the ride. Can't smoke before a gig, wrecks the throat, especially grass. Probably save me from lung or throat cancer.

In and out. Hired gun rides into town and rides off again. Neat and clean, no connection, no need to know the bloody aftermath. Sometimes later they'll send you a review. Never did get Ithaca that way before. Always wanted to connect, take a chunk or a memory with me.

In the rearview mirror I can see the lights on the hill. Can't make out the bell tower. Ah Cornell. So many memories. So many more embarrassments than triumphs. I wonder if it is always that way.

There's a light up ahead. Middle of nowhere. Red. Should be green by the time I hit it. Candor. That's right. Just before the accident. Wonder if they survived. Drive carefully, boy.

The mayor of Candor lies.

Great line. No, not that great, good. Living in Candor. The light is green, an invitation to zip on by. I slow. See once again the streetlight. Notice again the sign. Written only on one side. I wonder why. The crossroad leads off to the right, nothing on the left except a farm. What the hell, can't be far. I turn right into Candor.

A church on the left. Then a warehouse. Then houses on both sides. A bridge. A store. A bar on the right. Then more houses, all shut tight. It's past midnight. The main road bears off a 45 degree angle to the left where even though a smaller road continues straight, I bear left. A post office, another two churches, a big feed grain elevator and a library. A little nothing town, saddled with the name Candor.

I turn left again, back over another bridge. I'm headed back to the main road. It's really dark. The houses, except for an occasional porch light, look neat but abandoned. Like one of those science fiction stories about whole populations being wiped out by a mysterious virus. I hit the main road, turn right and leave Candor behind.

The phrase repeats itself. It sticks. I feel a story song coming on. By now I know the symptoms. Look for the hook. The interesting twist that makes the musical journey worthwhile. Ok, the mayor of candor lies—but what about? And to whom? My mind starts working. The cigar burns. I pull out a pen and start writing on the Avis courtesy waste bag that dangles from the glove compartment knob. I don't slow to write. A superstition with me by now. I find if I stop to write down what I'm coming up with it vanishes. So instead I scribble in the dark on the seat beside me. Later I will translate the scrawlings into something that hopefully makes sense.

I'm through Binghamton and 75 miles down 17 when I pull over at an all-night diner. Then the euphoria takes over. I've got it all figured out. So neat. So startling. So dramatic. Of course my weakness as a writer is that every new song is the best I've ever written. But still I know it starts to feel damn good.

For me there are three parts that go into the creation of a song. One and three are easy. The first is the general idea. You know, "Why don't I write a song about....?" Everybody has that kind of general idea. No magic there. The third is the technical skill to bring the song home in a polished way. That is also an available step, although it takes practice and work. Still, an available ingredient.

The second part is the most important and also the most difficult one. One that seems to be my own particular version. One that makes a "story song" different, if not compelling. The second part is the conceptual bridge. That brings a song full circle. That ideally renders the conclusion not obvious, but inevitable. Could call it the payoff. And hopefully the payoff contains a verity, a truth.

In that diner, between New York and Binghamton at almost three in the morning I thought I knew about Candor, the Mayor, and the song.

That, and three cups of coffee, got me home.

Searching For the Mayor of Candor

Heading up to Candor, New York, I make a stop along the way at Warner Stoker's Stoves and Coal. I am going to Candor to see if I could find the mayor, if there is one, and Stokers Stoves seems like a good place to find some Chapin fans. Which it is.

I meet Jessie Clifford and his wife, Anna, and I ask them what they thought of Harry Chapin. They're down from Syracuse, New York to visit relatives in Candor.

"Oh, I think if he was here nowadays, I think the kids would really like him, especially college students. I thought he was great," says Jessie Clifford. "I have all his music. And when Harry passed away we all started to listen to Tom Chapin."

"He was the epitome of America," Anna, a cashier at Wegman's supermarket, adds. "I think he told stories of everyday people and the experiences that he saw that went unnoticed by us. We could have been sitting in the same restaurant in Watertown and not have seen the same thing that he saw in that waitress's story. I really miss him.

"I'm going to start crying thinking about it. I remember right where I was when I heard he passed away. I was right underneath the stop light at South Bay Road and it came on the radio that he had passed away, and I just cried and cried and cried. It still brings tears to my eyes thinking about it. We didn't go a day without listening to Harry."

Soon, I'm back on the road to look for the mayor of Candor. As in the song, I find he's not at his office.

"In the little town of Candor
In the last year of my youth
I learned the final lesson of the
levels to the truth....

I go to find the mayor to work out
what I can but he's not at
his office...."

A sign up ahead says, "Welcome to the Village of Candor."
The Village of Candor has a population of about 900 people.
If you wanted to buy a house there now, it would cost you
about $79,000. There's not much work there though, and the
biggest event is the annual Fourth of July parade. That's about
it, except for the annual wood carver's show that the Candor Fire
Department hosts.

My first stop is at Joe's Delicatessen on Main Street to talk to
some of the local folks. "I remember this one man who came
into the store, and he told me that he came all the way from
California just to see the town of Candor after hearing that song
Harry Chapin had sung about it. He wanted to come to the
town of Candor just to see it," says David Pantle. "Can you
imagine that? I believe it was last summer."

"Is there actually a mayor of Candor?" I ask him as he stands
behind a cold cut counter.

"Yes there is a mayor.

"Is there a City Hall here in Candor? A place where he sits at
or an office where I can find him?"

"We have the Village and the Town Hall. The Village Hall
is over there by the library, around the corner on Main Street.
That's where their offices are, and the Town Hall is straight up
on the right-hand side. They just built a new building down
there."

I ask him if he ever heard Harry Chapin's song, "The Mayor

of Candor Lied."

"No. I never did, "he says.

An older gray-haired woman, who says she has been living in the town of Candor all her life, gets into the conversation. She says that Harry Chapin once got a speeding ticket driving through Candor.

Asked when he got it, she says, "Oh, I'd say it was shortly before the song came out. That's why Candor is mentioned in his song."

Another customer, Bob Spaulding, is sitting in a booth near the front window next to Main Street. After I introduce myself and tell him what I'm doing, I ask him about Candor and what people do here for a living.

"I was born and raised in Johnson City when we had the Endicott Shoe factory that used to employ about 20,000 people," he says as he describes the industry that once thrived here. "Now it's gone, and a lot of those jobs haven't been replaced with good paying jobs. IBM has moved out and they employed a lot of people at one time, too. I spent a lot of time in Athens, Pennsylvania, which is just about 30 miles from here. It's a small town but we had an Ingersoll Rand Plant that used to employ about 800 to 1,200 people," he says. "It's probably less than 300 now. That's the way the whole area is. You can buy a house here real cheap. It's really depressed. Years ago, the Lehigh Valley Railroad used to employ 3,000 men. That's gone too."

A man sitting in a booth in front of Bob Spaulding tells me that the Mayor of Candor is a man named Chad Showers.

I ask him how I can find him.

"Well, he's right in the phonebook. He might be down at the Village Hall, but I don't know if they are open today. They're on Main Street."

Driving down Main Street looking for the Village Hall, I pass American Legion Post 90, a one-story plain building that looks like it's been here for a long, long time. On the front lawn, there is a huge, old antiaircraft gun. Not far from it is the Loft Diner.

I walk in and start talking to three young people sitting at a table, a girl who is a waitress here, another girl, and a guy. After a while, I tell them that after walking around the town of Candor it seems like paradise to me compared to some towns I've been in. The three of them stare at each other and then back to me.

"Not really," one of them, Daryl, says. "What good is it if there's no work?"

Candor is a part of small-town America, part of something that existed a long, long time ago, but is fading fast. That's why when you drive into one of these towns it sort of surprises you. It's a place made up of local churches, Baptist and Catholic side by side, a library, the Town Hall, like something you would see on the layout of a Lionel Train town.

That's the sort of a feeling you get. Those little Lionel train towns of course were once based on towns like this, because once they really existed, and Candor is proof that they did. No doubt, Harry Chapin saw this many times as he traveled through here and put it in his songs.

I ask Daryl if he's working.

"I have a repair shop in Owego. We repair automobiles and trucks," he says.

"So I guess you won't be leaving Candor."

"Yeah. Guess not. Born and raised here, probably die here."

"Not much industry up this way anymore."

"No. There's not."

"Does it force a lot of young people out of town?"

"Yeah. It does. They're all going down south, Arizona, the Carolinas, Florida. You can go down South and make maybe ten dollars more an hour than you would here doing the same thing. Less taxes."

"What sort of work is around here?"

"Construction, maybe. Unless you're hired by Lockheed Martin over in Owego. They just got the helicopter contract. Work in a diner; maybe, concrete work. It's just an average town with average people, average work. Nothing big here."

He sits at a table with the two young girls, the waitress and the other girl. Other than me, there is only one customer this afternoon, so there's not much for the waitress to do. He sits at the table talking to the girls and drinking coffee. The three of them look like they're caught in a scene from an Edward Hopper painting.

As I walk out the door of the diner, I stop to look at a posting on the cork bulletin board. It reads: "Trailer for Rent. Town of Spencer, Nice Two-Bedroom Trailer. Small, quiet park New Carpet. $450 a month."

I pull up in front of the Town Hall, which is right next to the Grace Bible Church, a Baptist church. The only other structure around is a huge corn silo off in the fields, and then nothing but long stretches of open land with huge mountains in the background and clouds rolling by the blue sky this chilly afternoon.

I'm looking for the mayor of Candor. Instead, I find the Town Clerk, Carolyn Roberts. She sits behind her desk on the other side of a counter as you walk in. Just across the room is the Town of Candor Courtroom. It is dark and empty this day. I tell her that I'm looking for the Mayor of Candor.

"If you want to talk to the Mayor his office is down in the village," she says.

I tell her that I was just down there and a sign in the window said that they closed at two o'clock.

I mention the Harry Chapin song, "The Mayor of Candor Lied" to her, and ask her if she knew who the mayor of Candor was when the song came out.

"William Muir was the mayor at that time. He's been dead about 20 years or so."

Did you ever listen to any of Harry Chapin's music?

"I went to his concert at the Broome County Arena in Binghamton in June, just before he died," she says.

I ask her if she ever heard "The Mayor of Candor Lied."

"Sure," she says. "My husband met Harry in a local bar when

Harry came up here. The Village Bar and Grill. Closed now, but it's still here. I don't remember the time frame, but he came home that night and told me that he spoke to Harry Chapin personally."

I mention to her that Harry didn't drink, and she says, "He probably just stopped to talk to Candorites. That's probably what he was doing there."

She talks about the mayor of Candor's reaction to Harry Chapin's song, a song about the local mayor sleeping with the narrator's mother, a song that some say is about incest.

"Muir thought that it was kind of funny. But at first he was very embarrassed by it." She pauses, and then she says, "William Muir, the mayor of Candor, was a part-time minister."

Leaving Candor, heading toward Route 94B North to Ithaca, I can see all around me evidence of a lost America. Back on Main Street in Owego, which I just rode through, they still have an ancient movie house where kids once spent cold, winter afternoons watching double features and ten cartoons for a quarter. Here and there, you still see a Rexall Drugstore, signs for stores that sell wood-burning stoves, and out in the open fields the silver tops of grain silos shine in the sun. Up ahead of me, a tall-gated open-back truck piled high with fresh cut logs creaks as it sluggishly moves past a country cemetery. And it all rolls by me like the pages of an old Texaco road map.

Old College Avenue

"It's funny about my memories
of Cornell. I miss it whenever
I'm away, but whenever I go back
I'm still remembered by enough
people and I hate it, or remember
how I hated it when I was here.
I do have fond memories of my
double bed though. It was the
best bed in the whole wide world,
and all the good things that happened
to me at Cornell happened in that bed. "
                        —Entry from a spontaneous,
                        unpublished diary that Harry
                        Chapin wrote in the early '60s
                        near Plattsburgh, New York.

OLD COLLEGE AVENUE

 "Of course I picked a rainy night
To try to find our past
The streetlights all were flickering
The leaves were falling fast....
It was Old College Avenue
And in time of having you
I remember it as if it was today...."

I'm headed into downtown Ithaca, up the hills to College Avenue. Seeing Cornell University for the first time leaves you with a sense of awe. College Avenue, like the yellow brick road, leading up to the massive front gates that appear to usher you into an education Land of Oz.

The streets are filled with energy that you can feel as you watch young college students move through them. They come from all over America, all over the world to experience an education that comes with a big price tag.

And you know that most of them are the best we have in this country, or they wouldn't be here. Their faces are young and filled with dreams, and you don't want to think about how many of those dreams might die.

A huge neon sign that hangs above a store front, rusted now, displays a red cartoon bear in a college T-shirt with a big "C" on it. Bulbs that once lit up the words, Johnny's Big Red Grill, are long extinguished. The sign is enormous, about 16 feet long, and it hangs onto the side of the building and out over the sidewalk. Nobody mounts signs like this anymore. *Too bad*, I think. It will hang there like a memorial to another time for years to come, because removing it would be costly. Part of the brick front of the building would probably come with it.

Johnny's Big Red Grill has been closed since the '80s, and you have to wonder how many dreams ended here on dark wintry Saturday nights when drinking lost its fun. In 1964 Harry Chapin, at 22, played guitar in Johnny's Big Red Grill. Some older townies who drink in the remaining old saloons say they remember him also playing piano there. True or not, it's an image that lives on in their minds.

I have driven here from Candor, chasing after the ghost of a young Harry Chapin who once walked down College Avenue with a guitar case in hand and a stack of dreams. College Avenue is the street where he wrote a lonely song about Jenny Gillette, a Cornell student, and former love. Just around the corner from College Avenue, and across the street from Johnny's Big Red

Grill is another Ithaca landmark, The Royal Palm Café. It has stood in the same spot on Dryden Avenue since 1941.

Cornell students call it "The Palms." The place is empty this fall Monday afternoon except for the owner, Joe Leonardo, who pours me a pint of Budweiser.

He describes Johnny's Big Red Grill for me. "It was all one area. It wasn't divided up in the middle like it is now." (It has been boxed off and turned into two different Asian restaurants) "There was just a little bar on the side where the noodle shop is now. A small bar, probably only ten feet long. The kitchen was in the very far back. All on the bottom floor."

"Do you get mostly Cornell students drinking in your place?" I ask him.

"That's all I get, except for a few townies during the day or after work. Half of my townie crowd is former graduates from Cornell University. They came to Cornell to go to school and stuck around in town. They never went back home again."

I ask him what kind of work they found here after that expensive education at Cornell, and his answer to me is like the lyrics of Billy Joel's "Piano Man."

"There's a girl who comes in here who became a real estate agent, a guy who comes in who is a carpenter, and another who owns his own business as an electrician. And there's another guy who graduated law school at Cornell. But he doesn't practice law.

"There are a lot of people here that love Ithaca. When they get here to go to Cornell they want to stick around." He says that up until about five years ago they had an old jukebox in the bar and that "Harry Chapin was always on our jukebox... 'Cat's in the Cradle' was very popular up here."

Asked how long the Royal Palm has been here, he says, "This bar was opened up in 1941." Pointing out the window to Johnny's Big Red Grill: "They were here before us, before 1941. Whenever they hear 'Cat's in the Cradle' on the jukebox somebody will say that guy went to Cornell, he used to sing over at Johnny's Big Red."

A former Cornell student-who-never-went-back-home walks in. The owner points him out; his name is Bob, and he went to Cornell when Harry Chapin used to play across the street.

He's old now and a bit nervous as he pauses to get a first gulp of beer before he starts talking to me. His sports jacket looks sort of worn and old and his face tells you he's seen a lot of bad luck in his time.

He remembers seeing Harry Chapin playing at Johnny's when he was a student himself, but he doesn't remember all the details.

"I came here in '52. Yeah it was '52 when I came to Cornell. I never left. I work there now as a researcher." He was originally from Saranac Lake. "A lot of people come here and never leave." He picks up his beer with a shaking hand. Asked if he ever saw Harry Chapin walking around College Avenue, he says, "I think so, but I don't remember very much about it."

"Did you ever see him perform?" he's asked.

"Over at Johnny's. I used to go in there occasionally; more often I went here."

He remembers this about Johnny's: "Actually they didn't have that much entertainment. Mostly it was a restaurant with a very small bar. And there were no stools at the bar. I guess Johnny didn't want people hanging around like that.

"It was not a bar like this one where a lot of students came. There was very little of that. There wasn't much room for a drinking crowd. I would say about 20 people or so. It was later that they started having entertainment with, what's his name? Uh, what is his name, from Peter Paul and Mary? Peter Yarrow. He used to perform there. He went to Cornell too. Johnny's was an Italian restaurant then."

He describes the crowd at Johnny's for me that he remembers in the '50s, "Some professors, generally—older than a student crowd."

As we talk, another old-timer who passed through Cornell comes into the bar. He sits down at the very end of The Royal Palms, a bottle of Corona in his hand. He's a tall blond-haired man with a ponytail sticking out from his baseball cap. With a soft smile, he says his name is Tom Torrens.

Asked what he thought of Harry Chapin's music, he reflects, "It was representative folk music of the time. You know what I mean? A little bit critical of what was going on and hopeful that things would get better. But that taxicab song was kind of a bleak one.

"But I think he was a realist. We had some shaping up to do, but we haven't done it yet. In fact we could be backsliding." He laughs gently.

When I ask him what he thinks of America today, he says, "We got our heads up our ass. Looks like it will take a long time."

He says he liked Harry Chapin's taxicab song because "it spoke to expectations, and realizing what could have been and what might have been. Great song. I enjoyed his music and I thought he fit into the genre of his time, but I don't know what he would think about what we're faced with today. I don't know."

In some regards, to fail is not really a disgrace in America; people just shrug at it, go on and do the best they can. Why not? And yet, Americans can be puritanically tough on failure.

Asked if he ever hears anyone in town talking about Harry Chapin, he says, "No, not really. There are so many people who come through this town; Harry was one of them. A valuable one, but it was a long time ago that he was around here."

When I ask him what type of work he does, he looks me straight in the eye, pauses, and chuckles. "I'm unemployed. I'm a truck driver, a retired truck driver. Let's say that. I came down here to go to school at Cornell. But I fell in love with trucks. Yeah, I'd rather shift gears than sharpen a pencil." A smile opens his face, and he laughs again softly as he picks up his beer.

But then the door to his face suddenly shuts as he is asked where he came from before Cornell. He waves his hand at me as he says in a friendly manner, "That's enough. This is not about me. If you want to hear about Harry Chapin, good, but I'm nobody."

But you know he is more than that. He's part of the America you find in Harry Chapin's songs.

The Royal Palm Tavern is a huge, cavernous bar in which all kinds of dates, going back to the '50s, are carved into a row of wooden tables. Who knows, maybe they're even the names of the men I interviewed when they were young.

I look down on these chiseled monograms as I walk out the door, imagining pitchers of beer passed over the heads of students, almost hearing the noise and laughter of the room in some long-ago time when the men and women who carved their mark here seemed forever young, and a student named Harry Chapin was playing guitar across the street at John Petrillose's old place, Johnny's Big Red Grill.

His first gig.

Cats and Dogs

1. SANDWICH, MA
and "Cat's in the Cradle"

"The great thing about Sandy that
nobody seems to know is that she
wrote the poem *Cat's in the Cradle*.
and everybody said that's about
Harry and you. She had three children
before she married Harry. Everybody
thinks it's about Harry, but it's about
her first husband."
>   —Harry Chapin's dad, Jim. From
>   a radio show I hosted on WGBB,
>   Long Island called "Night Thoughts."

On my way to Gloucester, up through Cape Ann, I'll take the
long seashore roads and the old US routes as long as I can. I'm
in no hurry. I stop in Cape Cod in a little seashore town called
Sandwich.

Heidi, now in her forties, has lived in Sandwich all her life.
Her husband Jim is the local locksmith. She works out of a
family-owned small building, part craft shop, part hardware
store. Before it became a hardware store, it was Cape Cod's first
Catholic church in 1830.

CAT'S IN THE CRADLE

"And the cat's in the cradle and
the silver spoon
Little boy blue and the man
in the moon
When you comin' home, dad?
I don't known when, but we'll
get together then, son
You know we'll have a good
time then..."
—Lyrics by Sandy Chapin

"When I was younger I really didn't like the song 'Cat's in the Cradle,'" she tells me, "but when I got older, I realized that it's the God's-honest truth with a lot of people."

"How did you find that out?" I ask her.

"Through living. That's how you find most things out. Kids turn out just like their fathers. The fathers don't have time for children today. They're too busy playing golf. In my generation, the father was always out being the breadwinner. But today, they want their own life.

"They have Saturdays and Sundays off and they want to go play golf. Push the child aside. That's what they do. It's the God's-honest truth."

2. DOGTOWN

**"Up in Massachusetts there's a little
spit of land. The men who
make the maps, yes, they call the
place Cape Ann. The men who
do the fishing call it Gloucester
Harbor Sound, but the women
left behind, they call the place
Dogtown…"**

I drive over the Sagamore Bridge and pick up Route 3, the old Pilgrim's Highway, and head toward Gloucester to a place called "Dogtown."

In an 1858 entry in one of his journals, Henry David Thoreau, who hiked there, described Dogtown as "the most peculiar scenery of the Cape, its hills strewn with boulders, as if they had rained down, on both sides." A painter in the early 1900s named Marsden Hartley, a well-traveled man who had spent some time with Gertrude Stein in Paris in 1913, summed up Dogtown in a letter to a friend in 1931: "a place full of magnificent boulders driven and left by the glacial pressure of years ago… an eerie place, druid and savage in appearance."

Decades later, these descriptions of Dogtown still hold true. Remarkably, not much has changed. Sandy took Harry up there once and he walked out with an epic song that captures all that Hartley tried to paint during his frequent visits.

When I walked in the door of a local Gloucester shop, "Cats in the Cradle" was playing on the radio. A good sign I thought. Chris Walsh, who runs it, gave me a brief history: "At one time, Dogtown was the part of Gloucester that was settled, but as the seashore became safe and wasn't attacked by the British, people started moving closer to the coast.

"But the poor couldn't leave, the widows from the war, they

ended up staying there with all the dogs. These women and their dogs became the settlement of Dogtown. So it became known as a place where witches and werewolves reside."

"And the men?"

"There were a few. It had a very colorful history, a lot of speculation about whether they were warlocks, male witches."

Asked if she ever went up there, Chris says, "I have to be honest: I never had the opportunity to go there because everyone said don't go by yourself. I like to mountain bike, but everyone says 'not alone.'"

Good advice. I later found out that about 20 years ago a woman was attacked by a psycho with a sharp rock who was wandering around Dogtown. He left her to die in the pouring rain, propped up against a boulder. After the story hit the local newspapers, Dogtown remained empty and desolate.

The main entry into Dogtown is at Cherry Street. You drive down a dirt road, and at the end of it, there's room for only a few cars. Doesn't matter, not too many people come here. I was told to lock mine up.

I spent about two hours hiking around there on a sweltering, summer afternoon. Once you reach the end of a gravel road, it gets very confusing: mostly rock and hills and half-paths seem to take you nowhere. Every now and then, you come across a rock into which a man named Roger Babson carved inspirational sayings in the 1920s, like "Never Try, Never Win." It's an odd place to find inspirational sayings.

Babson also numbered rocks in front of sites that were once the homes of the women of Dogtown. I found several of these fading numbers. It gives you a chill, standing in front of one. You can imagine what it must have been like when the night would come here, and rain storms would blow through, exhausting the camp fires and all those women with only the dogs for company would settle in.

Somehow, Harry Chapin caught all the grim history of this place in a song, almost as if he had lived it—another example that distinguishes him as one of our greatest American songwriters. Unfortunately, in the world of musical awards, he still hasn't received his due. His true musical genius as a writer, composer, has gone unnoticed for too long.

"All these grey-faced women in their widow's gowns living in this graveyard granite town, you soon learn there's many more than one way to drown. That's while going to the dogs, here in Dogtown..."

The writer part of me was glad to visit Dogtown, but another part of me was thrilled to get back to my car and over the crushed stone road where I left it.

Rock 'N' Roll in a Backstreet Bar

I have crossed the width of Massachusetts in two and a half hours, and now arrive in the northern part of New York State's Hudson Valley. Herkimer, cleaved by the Mohawk River, is my first stop on the way to Watertown. Herkimer is named after Nicholas Herkimer, a general who was killed in battle during the Revolutionary War. The town is known for its diamond mine and the Remington Arms Company that has been here as long as anyone can remember. For decades, this diamond mine and bullet-making factory had been enough. But that changed.

I stop in a place called the Baby Boomer's Lounge. It's kind of quiet tonight, so I get a chance to have a beer with the owner, Gordon Turner.

"I've lived in Herkimer for 49 years. I was born here," he says. "My wife and I opened the bar about 8 years ago."

Asked what sort of work most Herkheimers do, he says, "The biggest employer is Remington Arms over in Ilion. But they're downsizing, like everyone else. They used to make Remington typewriters there. The typewriter parts came from Ohio, back in 1936 or thereabouts. They went on strike out there in Ohio so Jimmy Rand moved his whole factory to Ilion.

"My grandfather worked for Rand and when they went on strike, a lot of folks just went with him to Herkimer. He brought along the ones he wanted. That's how a lot of people came here from Ohio."

"How's business in Herkimer nowadays?"

"Slow. Back in the '60s Herkimer was booming. You had Mohawk Data Science. You had big computer companies. I think it was IBM who broke off and started MDS. I mean, a lot of people who invested $10,000 in it became millionaires a year later."

He describes the type of work they have around here now.

"County jobs. They pay good. They give good benefits, but there isn't a lot of employment for someone young here unless they can start something themselves. A lot of people wind up just leaving town."

We drink some beers together at the bar and after a while I tell him that I am heading up to Watertown, New York, a place that Harry Chapin wrote a song about.

"What was that song with the barmaid in it that he wrote up there?"

"'A Better Place to Be,'" I say.

"Yeah. I'll have to look it up. I play guitar and I have a lot of song books," he says. "A bunch of us just jam in here some Saturday nights after the place closes. There's this guy Chancy that comes in here. That's what we call him. He was part of the group The Happenings who did 'See You in September.' And he'll come in and sit at the bar and harmonize. Oh, what a beautiful voice he has. And that was The Happenings, a lot of harmony. I don't know how he wound up in Herkimer. And I don't ask. He sells engraving machines now, sells them to jewelry stores.

"Bill Haley's Comets came in here one night. This was about four years ago." (*He points to an autographed picture on the wall of the current members of Bill Haley's Comets.*) "They were playing a policemen's benefit down in Little Falls, and they called me up. Jesus, what a hell of a night that was. I'll never forget it.

"It was about 10:30 when they called. And one of them says , 'We're coming up to eat', and I said, 'Well, the kitchen's closed.' So he says, 'Look, we just did this police benefit and we want to stop somewhere to get something to eat and drink.' A little while later, I get this call from one of the policemen down there who

I know, so we had all this food ready for them when they came. They filled up the whole bar...

"Was just my chef and me here at the time. So we all got talking, and I had my guitar and I brought it out. They had one guy who was the designated driver, drinking coffee. Everybody else was drinking beer."

"Did they tell you who they were when they called?"

"No, I don't think they did. We got talking about the guitar, so we just passed it around. Everybody who was at the bar would play a song and everybody would sing. It's like there were 13 people, one guitar and 13 people. Everybody was harmonizing. That's about all I play is old songs. "

He points back up at the picture. "I think only one of them actually played with Bill Haley, and that's "Bam Bam," the drummer, the guy in the center." (*John "Bam Bam" Lane worked with Bill Haley from 1965 to 1968.*)

"He told some road stories that night about how they were on a bus once; they were out West somewhere. You know back then, a lot of guys that worked with Bill Haley would be hired, they would play for a few years, and then they would hire someone to take their place. (*Bill Haley actually stayed on the road until his death in 1981.*) Well Bill Haley found out that this one guy had pot on him, so he just stopped the bus, and threw him right off into a field. And he said, 'You're fired.' (*Laughing.*) And they just drove on, and when they got into town, Bill Haley found someone else to take his place. That's how they worked."

He talks about how they all drank late into the night at the bar, telling musician road stories. "Because we stayed open for them, one of them went and got the band picture and they all signed it. That one guy up there, I can't make out his name, and I don't remember it, but he told me that he went down to Tennessee and he wrote songs for other singers. He's in his 60's.

"Some of them are famous songs that Country and Western singers played...But he's just a name on a piece of paper now. That's the way it goes.

"Another time, Danny and the Juniors came in here one night and it was the same type of a deal. They were playing at a sheriff's fundraiser in Herkimer, and came here afterwards...I broke the guitar out, and we jammed."

I ask him how he feels about Harry Chapin and what his music was all about.

"His music told a story. That's why I always liked it. It wasn't just music. I think he connected with the workers. I always thought he was talking about people. And people are America.

"There's a guy who comes in here. I wish he was here tonight. He's a radio announcer and he has a show in Utica now. But when I was growing up he had a TV show here called 'Twist-A-Rama.' His name is Hank Brown. He was working out of Little Falls. I think it was WLFH. It was all AM back then.

"This was the '50s, '60s. I think he started the show in the '60s. It was a takeoff on American Bandstand. While American Bandstand was national, this was local. But he had different bands on there.

"He even had Neal Sedaka on once. He would be good to talk to about Harry Chapin's music. He comes in here every Friday night for fish. That's his night. Fish night. He's at WIBX now. Out of Utica. Where you headed?"

"Well, I'm staying overnight at a motel just down the road from here," I tell him, "and then in the morning I'm driving up to Watertown. After that, I'm going to grab the car ferry and cross over into Canada from Cape St. Vincent. I'm going to lie back for a while. Just take it easy."

"Well damn, if you take Route 5S into Utica you'll see a huge billboard with Hank Brown's face on it. "

"Well, I'll do that." And I did.

The next morning, on the way out of town I stop at a diner on the corner of Main Street. I sit next to John Slopnick, 51, who grew up in Little Falls, which is about six miles from here. Slopnick is a schoolteacher and a Harry Chapin fan.

"When we listened to Harry Chapin's music we felt like he was talking to us," he says. He remembers the innocence of the '50s, growing up in Herkimer, going over to Ilion to a bowling alley on Saturday night where the owner, Bill Brown, brought in bands to play. And you could slow dance to early rock 'n' roll in this bowling alley.

The two of us stare out the diner window at an empty Main Street. It's one of those gray, rainy mornings that seem even lonelier in small upstate towns.

"What's it like now, living in Herkimer?" I ask him.

"This town is typical of the area, Mohawk Valley. These little towns—Herkimer, Mohawk—they have all come upon hard times. The economy has shifted to elsewhere in the world and in the country. They're struggling to get their feet back on the ground.

"We used to have a lot of factories. Little Falls, six miles up the road, was full of factories. There was work for everyone. They had a bicycle factory, which ran for years until the mid-'70s, when it was bought out and closed. There were factories that made parts for automobiles. There was a huge shoe factory that closed. There was a factory that made wooden desks right here in Herkimer. They were all the way through the Mohawk Valley. Now they are all closed."

The Midtown Tavern on Main Street is a place that draws in early morning drinkers. Not much else to do, so you might as well play the jukebox and talk to friends. I join them. John, who was born in Little Falls, tells me he did a lot of window washing in New York City for about 18 years. He used to drive all the way down there to wash the windows of an old military armory in Brooklyn.

He says he heard that Remington Arms is building back up. "Maybe something will come of it. Who knows?" He shrugs his shoulders, drags from a cigarette with this ruined Johnny Cash face, as he offers out some hope in a husky voice. "Well, I take it day by day now. That's all I can do."

The two of us talk and drink beer in this dark long bar, lost somewhere in the slow-moving time of an old factory town upstate. It's only about 11 A.M., and I feel like I've been here for hours.

The brightest parts of Main Street in Herkimer, New York, are the red and blue neon signs that hang in saloon windows, advertising Genie's Cream Ale and Labatt's Blue. A big sign advertises "Brownies, the Valley's Only Real Night Club. Number One for Live Rock and Roll Since 1996." Farther up Main Street are a lot of For Rent signs in empty store windows.

Downtown, there is the General Herkimer Hotel, which has seen better times. Over at the corner bus stop two people stand with old suitcases in their hands. Looks like they're leaving town. The expression on their faces tells you that it might be for good. Behind them, a large poster announces the coming of a Baptist preacher to a church in town where he will speak on Saturday night. "All are welcome."

Well, that's two that won't be saved, I think.

Main Street is empty except for a couple of stragglers over in the Dollar Depot Thrift Store. Once, in better times, it was a

Woolworth Five and Dime. It still has the recognizable red front, facade design of all Woolworth stores across America. Up above it is the faded shadow of the missing, gold store letters.

In the front window is a large, ceramic head of James Dean for sale, the red plaster collar of his windbreaker pushed up as he stares out at Main Street. I'm sorry now that I didn't buy it.

The Day They Closed The Factories Down in Utica, NY

Utica, New York sort of haunts you with the memory of another time that seems to be everywhere. Few traces are left of the industrial revolution that birthed Utica. Nowadays the city has the mood of a Theodore Dreiser novel. There's nothing much left now but hope, and the lengthy dark of the harsh, cold winters that bear down on this city with the change of seasons.

Utica has become a part of the rust belt that runs as far north as Buffalo. Once in the '60 s there were over 100,000 people living here, many of them making a good living from the rows and rows of factories on Broad Street. Now Utica stands as testimony to one of Harry Chapin's story songs about the changes in America, like "The Day They Closed the Factories Down."

Today Utica's factories sit vacant as the wind blows through the broken windows and across empty loading docks. The population has dropped to almost half of what it once was. Many current residents are refugees who have come all the way from Africa, from the former Soviet Union, from Vietnam and Bosnia to settle in Utica.

They may have come "to look for America." But they're too late; the American Dream has left town. Rarely will you even see politicians pass through here, unless they're running for governor, or a camera crew, trolling out wire to a TV reporter— unless there's a murder.

The tool and die factories went first. They moved down south, leaving behind laid-off workers, empty saloons and gas stations that soon closed down. The biggest, and most famous, was the General Electric factory at 1001 Broad Street, which once sent over 8,000 people streaming in and out of its doors on different shifts. The factories ran 24 hours around the clock at times, nonstop even through holidays. General Electric gained for Utica the title "The Radio Capitol of the World." It was here that General Electric made some of the first portable radios in America.

But in the 1960s General Electric shut its Utica factory and moved to the Far East. The streets of this industrial area became more and more silent. I stop by and get out of my car to look up at its old front doors. I can feel the sort of loneliness that overcomes you in a cemetery.

At some point in its history, Utica, New York became known as "The City that God Forgot." There were so many people leaving that by the 1990s there were bumper stickers placed on cars that read, "Last One Out of Utica, Please Turn Out the Lights."

Driving down Broad Street on an early Sunday morning, I can see block after block after block of closed-down factories. The country music on my car radio suits the mood; gospel music now. Some group called the Sons of the Holy Water. This place could use some holy water. I turn it up loud.

Just before you enter Utica proper, you cannot escape these empty behemoths of another time in industrial America when life was simpler. I see red brick mills, many of them with windows broken and rusted, metal shutters swinging back and forth. Rows of smokestacks remain, even though their top tiers of bricks are shifting, some missing. Not a person around now. Stillness.

That morning rush hour, once made up of union label men and women and all the hope they carried with them as they walked through these great factory doors is just a memory now, boarded up inside forever. And no one who witnessed its destruction realized that one day soon it would even get worse in America.

As I drive down the deserted streets I now play a CD of Harry Chapin's, "The Day They Closed the Factory Down." He had an eye on what was happening. Too bad the politicians weren't listening, too.

THE DAY THEY CLOSED THE FACTORIES DOWN

"So they're moving somewhere else now
With their cloths and fabric press
They found themselves another town
Where they'll make shirts for less."

This story has been repeated all across what was once industrial America. In Flint, Michigan, GM found a place where they could make the cars for less. So they closed their factories and left town. In a city that once had 12 auto plants running day and night, there is only one now. And that too might be leaving soon.

It's all over for this part of America, I conclude as I drive on through the side streets. These factory towns will never come back.

What lives once played out here? I can see ghosts of factory men sitting on truck loading docks, sandwiches in hand, drinking a cold quart bottle of Genie's Cream Ale on some long-ago hot summer lunch hour when they were young. Once upon a time in America when it was easy to dream.

Once, even on cold Saturday wintry mornings, when work was what defined who you were in this country, these mills bustled with laborers, red-plaid shirted, with their black lunch pails in hand, leftover meatloaf from last night's dinner on a hard roll. Once, there came streaming out of these doors hundreds and hundreds of workers from morning shifts, factory whistles blowing in the cold air, walking to nearby taverns under slate gray skies.

Maybe it wasn't perfect. Factory work could be long and boring. But their wives and kids were safe at home, and it made all that hard work worthwhile. So much of what we are, and what America is, started in towns like this.

He saw all this, Harry Chapin.

"I Once Spent a Week in Watertown One Afternoon."

—Harry Chapin

In this chilly, seemingly forever-winter town with its murky skies, just a few miles from the Canadian border, I tried to find the bar from Harry Chapin's song, "A Better Place To Be." The gloom of Utica behind me now, I pull onto Route 12 North, and I head up toward Watertown, New York. If I have read my map right, Route 12 North will take me clear straight through. Ahead is a long ride through vast stretches of nothing but cornfields and wide plains that go on and on and on.

After witnessing the desolation of Utica, I find it clears my head. I can even imagine Harry Chapin taking this long, boring ride. It won't be long now until I am discovering what he meant by, "I once spent a week in Watertown one afternoon." As I look out at the sameness of the farms I pass, I'm starting to get the idea.

And then in the emptiness of it all, I see up ahead what looks like an old rural roadhouse. As I pass by I read the sign out front: "Midnight Madness Every Friday Night." And I think, how good they get some midnight madness up this way.

On the long stretch of 12 North, I pass in and out of rainstorms as I drive through the Adirondack mountain country. Above me is a sky filled with rolling black clouds. I'm on dry road now, but in a little while, I'll be back in the heavy downpour.

Entering Lowville, I notice Country Bob's Restaurant and the Lowville Diner. A sign outside says "Ham and Eggs, with coffee, $2.50." Food is cheap up this way. Nobody has a lot of money to spend. I see a sign painted on an old piece of wood by the side of the road: "74 Acres of Good Land for Sale."

And I think, *by God, if you were a man or a woman who wanted to get away from it all, get away from the city, you could come up here to these 74 acres of good country land, build a small home on it, and make that land yours. And on wintry mornings, you could go down to the Lowville Diner for some $2.50 worth of ham and eggs. With coffee.*

I drive on. Man up ahead herding cows across the two-lane highway and up a high hill. A whole lot of cattle. Dark clouds above, like an illustration from the America that existed in those grammar school readers, a Winslow Homer scene.

John Mellencamp is on the radio now, singing about how life goes on long after the living is gone. I glance out the window at the side of a hill that whizzes by: a group of rocks that spell out "Praise God." And I roll my window down and yell out, "Okay, I will!" I think in Jack Kerouac's *On the Road* that he did something like that after he saw a "Drink Coca-Cola" sign.

Then, of course, it was bound to happen. Even way up here. The ugly side of America catches up with me. A voice interrupts the music station I have on to announce that, "This afternoon a Home Depot employee turned on a bunch of fellow workers and killed all of them."

Put Mellencamp back on.

BROWNVILLE, NY, A TOWN BUILT FROM PAPER (THE GATEWAY to WATERTOWN)

I drive into Brownville, a small town very near Watertown. This place once depended mainly on the paper mill industry to drive its economy. I pull the car over and after walking around Brownville's few streets, I meet a man named Matt Brenon.

We get to talking about local life.

"There are still a lot of folks involved in the paper-making industry in this area. There's the Rexam DSI factory, which is one of the big mills here. The other one is Brownville Specialty Papers. Brownville was built on the paper mills. No question of that.

"A good portion of the mills in all of northern New York are going south, but there are some that are still kicking. Not many. It's a father-and-son thing. I know a lot of families where dad worked in the mills and the son followed in his footsteps. That's the way it used to be. "

He says he's a former DJ and that he used to do the "Saturday Night All Request Party" at WCIZ. They call it Z93 now, "Froggy Radio."

"We played rock 'n' roll, and pretty much of everything. A little bit of Bruce Springsteen, Don McLean, Harry Chapin. Harry Chapin says something on one of his albums about once spending a week in Watertown one afternoon." He laughs.

"Well that's why I'm up this way," I tell him. "I'm trying to find out who the 'fat woman' was in his song, 'A Better Place to Be,' and the name of the bar where it takes place."

He starts to talk about "WOLD," Harry's song about a DJ who tries to stay young by moving from radio station to radio station. Brenon knows about that life.

"'WOLD' is the DJ's hymn. I worked a Saturday night evening show from six to midnight. Our station was really popular in Kingston, Canada where they could pick up the signal. We played a lot of Harry Chapin stuff. Many of our requests came out of the Canadian side of the border.

"It was around the time of the cover of 'Cat's in the Cradle' by Ugly Kid Joe, and I can remember that being a number-one requested song for weeks and weeks on my all-request show. We were getting ten to twelve requests a night for that song from all over the place. I was called Mega Matt back then."

I ask him what he does now. He points to a bar across the street, Dundy's Tavern. "I run a company that provides video games and jukeboxes to bars all over northern New York. Dundy's is one of them. My father was in the same business. He provided pinball machines to the working-class taverns that are on the side streets of every upstate New York factory town. That's what we do. It's a family business that has been going on for over 50 years."

After we say goodbye I decide to stop in Dundy's Tavern where a bunch of unemployed construction workers sit around drinking tall neck bottles of Budweiser during the slow crawl of the afternoon. I join them. After a while we start talking about Harry Chapin and the loss of factory jobs up here. "I remember 'Cat's in the Cradle,' 'Taxi.' I thought 'Taxi' was good. Down to earth. It explained a lot of things," says Mike Taylor.

"A lot of the paper mills have gone. In the last year, four of them closed within 60 miles of here. Put a lot of people out of work," one of them says.

But they would rather remember the boom years in Brownville when they were younger and hanging out in places like The Candy Cane Lounge on a Saturday night, a local cocktail lounge. They talk about a singer named Danny Ardell who they say once played with Danny and the Juniors, and who used to manage The Candy Cane Lounge.

But when I check that name later, I find out that a man named Danny Ardell was the lead singer for The Del Vikings, and I find no record of his being in Brownville, New York. There seem to be a lot of tales of lost rock 'n' roll history up in these small factory towns, filled with stories of what might have been, and entertainers that got close, but never quiet made it to the top in New York City, and had to come back home.

Some stories seem true; some are just rumors, lost in the memory of men who drink in side-street saloons like Dundy's Tavern, never to be recalled again with accuracy.

Harry's revisions for the song "A Better Place to Be"

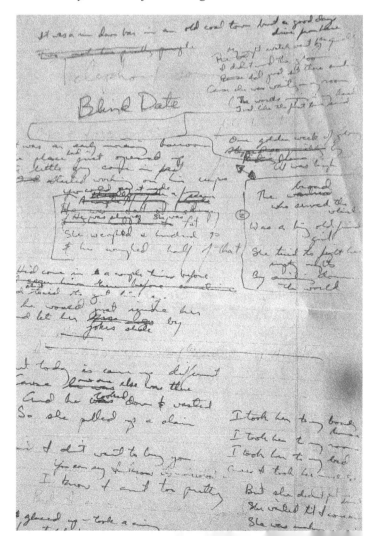

WATERTOWN, NY

A BETTER PLACE TO BE

"It was an early morning barroom,
and a little man came in so fast and
started at his cups.
The girl who sold the whiskey
was a big old friendly girl who
tried to hide her empty nights
by smiling at the world..."

When you drive through downtown Watertown, New York, the town seems to come at you in black and white: an old gray all-night diner, saloons, a local radio station, a fetid-looking Greyhound bus depot, a cab stand called "Fat Man's Taxi," and down the block a junkie sits on a bench in the middle of the Village Green just staring at the traffic rolling by.

I stop at the West Main Street Diner and order a ham and Swiss cheese sandwich to go. The woman behind the counter has a face that has seen a lot of trouble.

"We only have American cheese in here," she says."

And I say, "Well, American certainly is all right with me. As a matter of fact, I believe that I prefer American now that you mention it."

She stares coldly and says, "So you're just cruising around, aren't you?" I'm still not sure what she meant by that.

Over a cup of coffee, I talk to one of the locals, Charles Narrigan, who relives for me the day Harry Chapin came to Watertown and left behind the mystery of the fat lady in his song, "A Better Place to Be."

"I was still in high school then. I got out in '76. The concert was held at JCC Community College up here on the hill. Right over there." He pointed out the diner window. "It was actually the first concert that I ever went to."

"Had it been crowded?"

"Yeah. I'd say it was. The traffic was heavy that night. It was raining…so hard and I can remember we were waiting for our parents to come and get us. He was funny. One thing that I remember was that he was asking people in the audience when they first had sex. And one kid hollered out, 'I had it when I was 12.' And he answered back, 'You must have had it with yourself.'" Later, walking down the main street of Watertown, I stop at a locksmith shop, and I ask the owner if he remembers Harry Chapin playing in Watertown.

"You're looking for the woman he was writing about in the song about the midnight watchman. Right?" Word travels fast in a small town.

I tell him, "Yeah, that's right. And I'm trying to find the bar in Watertown where he picked up the story for the song."

"Rumor has it that she works down at Crystal's Restaurant and Bar. That's just a short way from here in the town square. You could walk it."

The main characters in the song, according to Harry Chapin, were a "midnight watchman at Miller's Tool and Die" and a barmaid, "a big old friendly girl."

"Supposedly, the woman in the song worked down there. Actually, she doesn't work there anymore. That's what I heard. A while ago, Z93 radio down on Mullins Street had some kind of a contest, and they were giving away tickets for a concert and they asked people calling in if they knew who the 'broad who served the whisky' was from the Harry Chapin song. And then some woman called in, and she told them that she worked in the Crystal down here."

I went by the Crystal Restaurant and bar at 87 Public Square on the main drag, but ironically, as if to keep any secrets it might hold to itself, it was on the one day they are closed—Monday. And I had to leave.

The Crystal is a bar-restaurant that has been serving up old-fashioned homestyle food like huge slabs of meatloaf with mashed potatoes since 1941. On one side of it is a long, dark bar that runs the length of the restaurant alongside some wooden booths. Peering through the front windows, I can see an old black and white tile floor.

It's located in the heart of downtown Watertown, across from the public square. When you think about it, you realize it would be a very convenient place for Harry Chapin and his crew to eat, and in which to sprawl out after a concert. And you can't miss the large sign out front as you drive down Main Street.

I go by the radio station, Z93 on Mullins Street, to see what they know about Crystal's.

"I haven't heard of Crystal's Bar," says DJ Lance Thomas. "I've heard of Coaches Bar and Allen's Diner. They used to serve liquor at Allen's years ago. That's the rumor—that this is where that big, heavy-set, friendly woman in the song is supposed to work.

"Our radio station ran a contest about two years ago to try to figure out who this woman was. We had a few women call in who said it was them." He shrugs. "Who knows, maybe one of those women was it. We may never know. But it's interesting that the song is still talked about and has become a legend here in Watertown."

Big Bob, another DJ, comes into the room and gets into the conversation. "Harry Chapin was bigger years ago. But being a classic hits station, we still play a couple of his tunes. Once in a while I'll just blow the dust off of it and I'll play the live cut of 'A Better Place to Be.'"

I ask him about Harry Chapin having the character in his song work at a place in Watertown called "Miller's Tool and Die."

"There were a lot of tool and die places in Watertown once. They served the nearby paper mills. There were guys working the tool and die shops 24 hours a day. So, the guy who did the third shift, he'd leave at 8:00 a.m. and stop off to have his drinks before he went home and went to bed."

"Still," I say to him, "he had to do some research to know about these tool and die shops to know about the different shifts."

"He was a great story teller," he says, "A blue-collar writer."

It's three in the afternoon, and I'm heading back to New York after one more stop in Canada. I put the radio on and tune in to the station that I just left, Z93, "Froggy Radio." Lance Thomas is kicking out the "Froggy Radio" call signs, and then I hear him say he was just interviewed by Pat Fenton who is writing a book about Harry Chapin. He says that today is the anniversary of Harry Chapin's death, so he's sending a song out to Harry and me, "A Better Place to Be." I turn it up loud as I pass by Crystal's Bar on the way out of town.

The Story of
Dwight "Skip" Johnson

BUMMER

"It ended one night in a grocery store
Gun in hand and nine cops at the door
And when his last battle was over
He lay crumpled and broken on the floor....
They found his gun where he'd thrown it
There was something else clenched in his fist
And when they pried his fingers open they found
The Medal of Honor.
And the Sergeant said: "Where in the hell did
he get this?""

The late morning Delta flight out of LaGuardia Airport in New York lifted up and after a long climb on this cold, windy day in October, started to level off. I was on a Sunday morning trip to Detroit to search for the story of the young black soldier who appears in the Harry Chapin song "Bummer."

At the end of my long journey of searching for Harry Chapin's America, Chapin's son Josh travels with me. It was Josh who first told me that the almost-ten-minute long song called "Bummer" that his dad had written about a young, black Vietnam veteran, was actually inspired by a real man named Dwight "Skip" Johnson. And that he came from Corktown, a neighborhood in

Detroit. So we went there looking for what we could find of his memory.

In 1968 Johnson was awarded the Congressional Medal of Honor, and just a few years after that in 1971, he was shot to death by a grocery store owner as he tried to hold up a store in the Corktown section of Detroit, where he lived. He was just 23.

One of our first stops in Detroit City after landing in Metropolitan Airport was to grab a cab to a bar in the Corktown section. It was once a blighted area of Detroit where they advised you to stay off of the street at night, but lately they say it is starting to get gentrified by "hipsters" moving in.

Dwight Johnson grew up in the E.J. Jeffries housing projects. Built in the early '50s, by the late 1960s it had become a neighborhood of drug dealers and addicts. Eventually most of the project was torn down.

A large sign outside of the Nancy Whisky Pub tells you that it has been on the same corner since 1901. There are no windows on the bar, and a big Irion gate guards its doorway. It has the look of an old speakeasy. The Teamsters labor leader, Jimmy Hoffa, used the old wooden pay phone booth in the bar as his second office, they say. It's still there as you walk in.

The neighborhood around it has a desolate feel to it—a long, lived-in feeling of many families, many generations living and dying here. You would think that a place this old would hold some of the oral history of Corktown.

We walk in and order some beers. On the long back bar of the Nancy Whisky pub, there are rows and rows of union stickers. One says: "God bless America's Millwrights Local 1102."

Saloons like this were once on the back streets of blue-collar neighborhoods all over Detroit. They were there to serve the weary assembly line workers of GM after they finished up a long afternoon shift fighting the endless boredom of the line.

Once in the 1970s GM employed over 80,000 of them. Whisky and beer went down easy after a long shift on the line. It helped to clear away the boredom until the next early morning ring of the Big Ben alarm clock, and then it would all start up all over again. The assembly line once ran all night. It ran while you were sleeping. It never stopped.

Strangers stand out in places like the Nancy Whisky Pub where all the regulars know each other by name. After a while the barmaid asks where we're from, and what brings us here. I explain the book I'm writing to her and how I'm searching for what is left of the singer Harry Chapin's America. I mention Dwight Johnson to her and ask if she ever heard of him.

"He came from Corktown and he won the Medal of Honor?" she asks. "No. I never did."

"You never heard anyone at the bar talk about him?" I ask her. "He was the first black soldier from Michigan during the Vietnam War to be awarded the Medal of Honor."

"No, never did," she says again.

Josh talks football with a young couple next to us at the bar. They both live in the neighborhood. After a while I ask them about Dwight Johnson, but they never heard of him either.

In the Harry Chapin song "Bummer," he's out of the Army awhile, and he can't really hold a job. After he attempts to rob a grocery store the owner shoots him.

When the cops come and find him dead on the floor, they open up his clenched fist and find his medal of honor in it. And one of the cops says, "Where in the hell did he get this?"

The actual grocery store was a market called Open Pantry at 9660 Greenfield Avenue in Corktown, just a few blocks from where Johnson lived. In real life when the detectives arrived on the scene and found Dwight Johnston dead on the floor, they looked in his wallet for ID, and they found a frayed white card that said, "The bearer of this card, Dwight Johnson, is a member of the Congressional Medal of Honor Society."

He didn't know what to do with himself after he came home from the Army. Jobs weren't easy to come by. And then after being home only a short time he was notified that he was being awarded the Congressional Medal of Honor. It didn't take long before the Army asked him to reenlist. They said, "You'd make a damn good recruiter, Dwight. You could help us bring those young fellows in to help fight the Viet Cong, help end the war and bring the boys home." So he signed up again, to work as an Army recruiter.

Soon he noticed more and more people demonstrating against the Viet Nam War, hippie types. They said it wasn't a good war. They said we shouldn't be there. And they let Dwight Johnson know that. And he became uncomfortable with his new job of recruiting young black kids into the service to fight the war. He went AWOL a few times and started drinking too much.

Once he was the local hero here in Corktown. He was asked to speak at American Legion dinners, the Lion's Club. And it didn't take long before he tired of hearing, "Let's give a really big, loud Corktown welcome to Skip Johnson, an American war hero."

But the applause got louder and the events got bigger. One night the Ford Motor Company gave a dinner for him at Detroit's Cobo Hall. It was quite a night. Over 1,500 people came to see Dwight Johnson, before he was even 23 years old. One of the guests who came all the way to Corktown that night was General William Westmorland.

President Richard Nixon invited Johnson to his inaugural. And now when you ask about him in Corktown's oldest saloon, The Nancy Whisky Pub that has been on the corner of Harrison Street in Corktown since 1901, they say they never heard of him.

The barmaid says to try the Gaelic League Club on the other side of the highway on Michigan Avenue; "a lot of old-timers go in there," she says.

So we take the long walk across the footbridge that leads over the highway to Michigan Avenue. On the way we pass Rosa Parks Boulevard.

The tap beer flows easily inside the Gaelic League Club. And the people along the long bar are friendly, but after a few pints of Harp and talking to the bartender, I realize that the story of

Dwight Johnson is one that few people know about. Nobody has heard of him in here either. I talk to a middle-aged black man, and when I finish telling him the story of "Skip Johnson", he seems surprised that he never heard it before. "But," he says, "you know, I'm not living here that long. About 20 years."

Sitting at the bar, I think back on the Rosa Parks Boulevard sign just down Michigan Avenue, and it makes me wonder why there isn't a street sign for Dwight "Skip" Johnson, maybe one over near where the Jeffries housing projects used to be. Yeah, he died holding up a grocery store; maybe that has something to do with it. He wasn't a perfect hero for some people, I guess.

Still, I think they should be teaching the story of Dwight "Skip" Johnson in the public schools of Detroit. His life after the war fell apart at a time when not too much was known about post-traumatic stress disorder and how to treat it.

They buried him in Arlington, not too far from the grave of President John F. Kennedy. Afterward, his widow fought for the pension she felt he was owed, and after about three years she won. He was issued a full pension with the same benefits as a soldier who was killed in combat.

Once, when he was young, he served as an altar boy. Once, when he was young, he became an Explorer Scout. Once, he was given the Congressional Medal of Honor by President Lyndon Johnson, who placed it around his neck at the White House. Somewhere between the few short years he was home from the Army something went terribly wrong with his life. And it started with a war.

And that too is a part of Harry Chapin's America—a sad history of a young black war hero erased in his hometown, as if it existed only on a blackboard.

*Pat Fenton
in Corktown*

Goodbye to GM in Flint, MI

One of the best ways to move around the America that is blue-collar Detroit and Flint, Michigan is to travel by taxicab. You can learn a lot from the drivers who see America through a different window.

She says her name is Constance, and she grew up in Flint. "My grandfather dropped out of high school and went to work at GM. They paid good money. He was able to buy a house—a small house, one bathroom. But it was his. I grew up in it. GM once built a whole town of them in Flint for the workers."

I ask her how long he stayed working the assembly line for them. "His whole life," she says. "Stayed there until he died."

"Now that most of the factories are closed down, where do people who drop out of high school in Flint go for jobs?" I ask.

"Nowhere," she answers. "I went to school in Flint. I was the valedictorian of my class. And I'm driving a cab for a living."

We're headed to a bar in downtown Flint on Saginaw Street to meet a writer and former autoworker, Ben Hamper. Josh had set up the get-together. Hamper spent most of his life working the assembly lines at the General Motors factories that once were the life's blood of Flint, Michigan. He later wrote a book about it called *Rivet Head, Tales from the Assembly Line.* When it came out one critic described him as, "a modern worker writer, proletarian journalist." *Rivet Head* invokes the assembly line at the GM Blazer/Suburban plant, and how Hamper and all the other "shop rats" survived the day-in, day-out boredom. Hamper also writes about how he witnessed factories close down, one by one, as GM moved on looking for cheaper labor, and how he got to know the singer Harry Chapin. In the '70s Harry Chapin did a series of benefit concerts in Flint to help the unions out, and also to help the writer Michael Moore, who had just started an underground newspaper called *The Flint Voice*.

When we get to the bar, called Churchill's, in the early afternoon, Hamper is outside smoking a cigarette. The three of us walk in and grab a wall table in the large back room where we can talk. Drinks are ordered: bourbon and coke for them, a pint of Stroh's, a Michigan blue-collar beer, for me.

"You wrote what I think is one of the best leads I have ever read in a story," I say to him: "'Dead rock stars are singing for me and the boys on the rivet line tonight.' You guys were listening to heavy metal music from a smuggled-in boombox that you plugged into an outlet in a water cooler near you."

"Well, yeah," he says. "I didn't like that kind of music, but the more I thought about it, I thought, you know actually long-haired type rock is perfect for what we are doing. I mean it wouldn't make sense for us to listen to Simon and Garfunkel on the rivet line."

We talk about Harry Chapin for a while, and I mention his song "The Day They Closed the Factory Down."

"You saw that happen here in Flint with GM," he begins. "In many ways that song resonates clear across America now. Harry Chapin was a visionary. Once the factories boomed in towns all across America, and when they closed they left devastation in their wake. And it don't look like they are ever coming back."

He takes a long drink from his bourbon and coke, and he talks about the profusion of work that once existed in the factories of Flint. Once it seemed like it would never end. "My old man was a horrible alcoholic, but he always worked in this town," he says. "He would work for a month or two, and then—due to drinking—he'd get canned. And he used to tell me, 'I just go across town to Chevy and start working.' He'd put in six weeks there and go on a bender and get canned. And then he would go over to Fisher Body and get work. So you could just move around.

"The majority of guys I worked with who graduated from high school didn't bother to go on any further because they knew they had the safety net of GM."

I ask about the plant he once worked in. "The truck plant is still here. But there used to be at least 12 functional GM plants in Michigan. I think there are two or three left. It started in the '80s with Roger Smith, his regime moving to Mexico, you know. And farther south looking for cheap labor.

"The plant I used to work in, although it is still functional, used to employ 7,000 people. It was like a city unto itself. And then they honed it down to robotics. I think maybe 1,800 are employed there now. Yeah, maybe 1,800."

He pushes his chair out and gets up. "You guys mind if I steal away for a smoke?"

No. Not at all.

As he walks toward the front door of Churchill's out onto Saginaw Street I can't help but wonder what he thinks about as he stands outside, just a short drive away from the plant he once worked in as a riveter. You see it from the highway when you're driving into Flint. Memories of misery mixed with the good times of a regular paycheck must live on in the minds of the people of Flint who once worked there.

He comes back in and the waitress brings another round of drinks.

"Do you ever drive by the old truck and bus plant you worked in?" I ask him.

"Oh yeah, I drive by all the time," he says. "And a wave of nostalgia comes over me. It's almost like a magnetic force that wants me to drive into that parking lot, you know."

"Do you ever get the feeling when that nostalgia wave comes over you that you want to work the rivet line just one more time?"

"I do in my dreams. A couple of times a week. Yeah."

He talks about growing up in Flint and the opportunities he once saw here.

"When I grew up in this town you knew that you always had the safety net, if nothing else worked out, you could always hire into GM, make a great wage, raise a family, have a nice house, maybe even two cars. Probably by 1980 that reality was no longer in existence for kids. And it certainly isn't now. That's why you see an upsurge in this area of desperation.

"We were part of the last generation that, if you didn't want to go to college, like I didn't, and you didn't have any lofty goals, you knew you could make a pretty good living working in the shop and bring home a giant company check. It's not around anymore."

Ben Hamper has seen a lot of change in Flint. He has watched the crime rate climb, the city's drinking water become polluted with lead, and he saw the once-great city of Detroit, the motor city, file for bankruptcy. He's seen the employment that GM once brought here decline from 80,000 workers to 7,200. And he's seen the population of Flint go from 200,000 people in 1960 to about half of that today. These numbers are similar to those in Utica, New York, after they closed the factories down.

"Didn't GM actually build a town for its workers called Civic Park?" I ask him.

"Yeah. I grew up in Civic Park. They once had such an influx of workers coming up from the south, and coming up with nowhere to live, so they built houses for them. My grandfather came from Springfield, Missouri and he put in a lot of years with GM."

"What are your feelings about blue-collar America today compared to the America you saw growing up in Flint?" I ask him.

"Certainly in this town opportunity has pretty much evaporated, unless you want to work for 'Taco Bell', you know. I mean you don't have the high-paying blue-collar jobs anymore. I can only speak for Flint, I guess. There was a time you could just walk in and get those good-paying jobs. That option is gone. It's been gone for 25 years, which directly parallel this town's rising crime rate.

"It's ravaged this town," he says. "The figures show every year that Flint is number one or two in murders, in gang violence, in rapes. The evacuation of GM has left no options for a lot of people like me. When I got out of high school I thought, 'I'm going to be a writer. I'm too good for the factory. I'm not going to be like my grandfather. I'm not going to be punching that clock. I'm made for better than that.' But after a while, about three years, well, you know, reality set in.

"But I had that fallback. Kids today in this town obviously don't have that option. What you see today, the blight and poverty, is a direct result of that," he says.

Another round of drinks comes out as Ben reaches into his pocket for his iPhone. He shows me a picture on it of his childhood home in Civic Park. Houses there once cost about $15,000 when GM built them. For the few families that are left in Civic Park, hanging on because they have no place to go, their houses are worth less than that.

"It's just four miles from here in Flint," he says. "The house is all boarded up now. That's all that's left of it. That was once a beautiful home, but like so many of them it's just gone now, you know? Just gone."

One thing you notice as you drive through Flint, Michigan for the first time is that there are a lot of highways and streets named after the car companies: Fisher Freeway, Buick Freeway, Edsel Ford Freeway, Chrysler Freeway. One of the archways over Saginaw Street has the name VEHICLE CITY on it. It's as if they were placed here with the belief that the car companies would be here forever.

Pat Fenton in Flint

HARRY CHAPIN

March 14, 1980

Patrick Fenton
21 Litchfield Ave
Elmont, NY 11003

Dear Mr. Fenton,

Thank you very much for your letter. I'm sorry
that I haven't gotten back to you sooner.

I am intrigued by your song idea and hope to
pursue it at some point. My schedule for the
spring is such that I will be away a good deal
of the time and hence wouldn't be able to
research the idea properly but I will have
my staff keep reminding me of this potential
project.

Sincerely,

Harry Chapin

HC/dr

EPILOGUE

"He spoke to my creative writing class in Commack, Long Island as a guest lecturer. I had no idea who he was. He spoke about his process of creating a lyric, creating a poem, how he gets an idea, how he expands it. Then he took his guitar about mid-way through the discussion and he started singing.

"I was just immediately mesmerized by his presence, by his attitude, by his personality, by his songs. I was just 17. I never heard of him, but later, I realized that I had heard the song 'Taxi.' But at that time when he was talking to us, I didn't realize it was him. He was wearing jeans and a flannel shirt, and he had part of a beard at the time."
—Former resident of Commack, Long Island,
from 'The Cheap Seats'

Heading to Metropolitan Airport in a cab, Josh and I are bone-weary after driving through the streets of Detroit and Flint in taxicabs, weary after walking the streets of those cities and drinking in their bars, but feeling good about the people we met along the way.

Many of them, as I anticipated, could have emerged from a Harry Chapin song—or inspired one. People like our young driver Constance, once valedictorian of her class. I'm starting to understand just how much Harry Chapin saw America through his writer eyes. I'm starting to realize that he knew the ordinary, which is everywhere, is really not ordinary.

Leaning back in the cab and looking out the side window as we start the almost-ninety-mile ride to Detroit's airport, which will take about two and a half hours, I start to think back on where I'd been and what I saw. Watching parts of Michigan roll by me, factories and suburbs, I was a long way from Gunther's Bar in Northport, Long Island where it all started on a rain-soaked night with Sandy Chapin and the band playing Hank Williams covers.

I have crossed over scores of those old steel bridges that look like they were designed from erector sets, and I've seen many back roads and side streets. Going into Canada from Cape St. Vincent to a remote place called Wolfe Island, the ferry was so small that they hung half of my car off the end of it with a steel cable. There were only two other cars on it.

I went to an old European-style inn to relax after a long road trip through parts of America that seems to be fading fast. At night, someone would play an accordion under my window, and I would fall asleep drinking wine and reading.

Another ferry that took me farther into Canada, to Kingston, was huge, and yet mine wound up being the only car on it. I stood by the car in a drizzle that felt good on my face, standing on the deck drinking a can of Budweiser beer as we passed foreign oil tankers nudging indolently down the St. Lawrence River.

Staring across the vastness of the St. Lawrence at the very edge of America going by me, I felt more understanding of the country that Harry Chapin wrote about. He had caught something in his story songs that just might take years to understand. All those small towns and cities that I visited radiated a sort of gray, dead-of-winter solitude, a quandary that haunts the past that they stir up. But in the end Harry Chapin's stories were always hopeful.

Chapin had the talent to put into plain language extremely profound thoughts about the America we know. These days, we are living in a very complicated, polarized nation, more divided than I have ever seen it. Along with that, many voices of the great sages of our time are silenced: it can feel as if there are no more Harry Chapins who can try to explain what happened to us, what is happening to us. There are no more Pete Hamills, no more Jimmy Breslins. There are no more James Thurbers or Jean Shepherds to make us laugh at ourselves. (I don't even know if that is allowed anymore, laughing at ourselves.)

And there are no more John F. Kennedys, no more Bobby Kennedys, and no more Martin Luther Kings, to help heal us. No more like Tip O'Neill, who was willing to sit down with Conservative Ronald Reagan to bring the country together. We can only hope that some new voices on the political scene will fill their void.

I have seen boarded-up movie houses, rusted railroad car diners, country churches, shuttered gas stations and crumbling factories on the edge of towns. I have passed by old country cemeteries on hills at the end of towns with quarter moons hanging over them, farmers herding cows across two-lane highways; I have driven past bowling alleys that some people still go to on Saturday nights for fun, all of it like sequences from a Sunday morning comic strip of the '50s.

Something happened here to the face of America that should make the next generation pay attention to the past. It matters. And Harry Chapin, like the writers Sherwood Anderson and Thornton Wilder before him, caught that America in his story songs forever. It's a little banged up, a little the worst for wear lately, but there are signs that some of it is still out there. I know because I saw it.

About the Author

Pat Fenton was born in Windsor Terrace, Brooklyn, on St. Patrick's Day. He left Manual Training High School in south Brooklyn at the age of 16. At 20, after several years of working on assembly lines in Brooklyn's factories, he pushed up his draft for the Army and served two years from 1961 to 1963 as a military policeman in Germany. He eventually received a high school equivalency diploma and went to New York Tech on the G.I. bill for several years.

After eight gritty years as a cargo loader at New York's Kennedy Airport, Fenton quit to take a civil service job as a court officer in Manhattan's courts, and to continue a freelance writing career as a journalist that has brought him publication in magazines and books, including the *New York Times*, *New York Newsday*, the *New York Daily News*, and *New York* magazine. He has worked as a New York City taxi cab driver, bartender, and radio host.

His account of his years as a cargo handler at Kennedy Airport, "Confessions of a Working-Stiff," was published in 1973 in *New York* magazine. The acclaimed piece, which led to an appearance on the David Susskind television show, was later republished in numerous anthologies and text books. His work has also appeared in the writing anthologies, *The Irish, a Treasury of Art and Literature*, and *the Book of Irish Americans*.

In 2015, his play, "Stoopdreamer"—which takes place in Farrell's, one of the last Irish working-class bars in Windsor Terrace, Brooklyn—was entered into Origin's First Irish Theatre Festival of 2015 and was nominated for five awards.

Acknowledgements

This book would not have been possible without the encouragement and help of the entire Chapin family, and Pegge Strella who manages the Chapin office in Huntington, Long Island.

Over the many years I have been writing and getting my by-line published in New York's daily newspapers and magazines I have learned that the best writers know the secret of making it look easy. Like my friend and mentor Pete Hamill once said to me a long time ago, "People who see me at the Lion's Head bar probably think it's a sweet, easy slide; they don't see me over the typewriter at five in the morning." It took me over 25 years to write this book (off and on, for reasons that would take up too much space here to explain), but my hope is that most readers will think the writing of it was "a sweet, easy slide."

Thanks to Sandy Chapin who was always there for me, and the same to Jen Chapin. I could write several paragraphs about what a help, what a friend Pegge Strella was to me. She too was always there to encourage me with her support, and to hit the "easy button" whenever she could. And thanks to Jason Chapin who stopped by my house in Massapequa one afternoon with a six pack of Brooklyn Beer and we spent the afternoon talking about *Searching for Harry Chapin's America, Remember When the Music*, and drinking the beer, and just chatting. Wonderful company.

Equal thanks to Tom Chapin, and to Josh Chapin who towards the home stretch of the book became my traveling companion, one of the best you will ever find. And after telling me a Harry Chapin story I didn't know, that the song "'Bummer' was about a real person," he put together a road trip for the two of us to fly to Detroit City to see if we could find any traces of this person's life. His name was "Dwight 'Skip' Johnson," a young Black war hero, and he grew up in the projects in the Corktown section of Detroit, Michigan. And like in the song, he was awarded the "Congressional Medal of Honor" and was later shot dead while holding up a grocery store not far from where he lived.

Thanks to Martin Tubridy for inviting me for lunch in his home in Connecticut where he told me the story of the "real" Mr. Tanner, and how he reacted when he found out that it was he that Harry Chapin was writing about in a beautiful song about hope and dreams.

And thanks also to Bob Ciesielski who told me the real story behind the song "30,000 Pounds of Bananas" from behind the counter of his roadside produce stand in Scranton, Pennsylvania. He knew it well because he and his family lived it. In real life, his cousin Eugene Sesky was driving the banana trailer that crashed on nearby Route 307.

I also got a lot of support from my daughter Kelly and my son Patrick, two of my biggest fans, who were always there cheering me on from the "cheap seats." And of course my wife Pat—no amount of words could describe the support and encouragement she gave me throughout my long road journey, except to say that for over 53 years of being married, she has been the first reader of my words.

And I thank Mike Grayeb from the Chapin Foundation who helped publicize the idea as the book developed. And to writer Steve Villano who, along with Jason Chapin, helped to guide it toward a publisher. In memory, thanks too to Harry Chapin's father, Jim Chapin, who appeared live on my radio show "Night Thoughts" for two shows. Later, off the air, I spent a half hour talking to him from my car in the parking lot. What he told me added much to my knowledge of his son's life and his relationship with him. I would also like to thank Harry Chapin's mother, Elspeth Hart, and the kindness she showed me when I interviewed her one rainy afternoon at her Brooklyn home.

For me, probably one of the most important interviews in this book is the one with Bill Ayres. A special thanks to him (and in memory, James Chapin). If any fan wants to know what

Harry Chapin was all about they only have to read it. It will tell them more than any detailed biography could. In an hour-and -a-half interview Bill, and at times with James Chapin, told me stories about who Harry Chapin really was, his weaknesses, his strengths, his kindness, and his deep desire to help others.

Bill Ayres, somebody that was one of the closet people in Harry Chapin's life, called up memories that showed how fragile the singer's life was at times, how troubled it could be, along with stories of humor, determination, and empathy for people who sometimes felt passed over. He told it in a way that only someone who truly loved him could.

I spent a lot of time in the seaside hamlet of Point Lookout, Long Island. Much of it was spent with one of the residents, Paul Gomez, who became a close friend to Harry Chapin, often taking part in music nights at Harry's home. I thank him for the time he spent with me as I searched for the story behind the song "What Made America Famous," and the way he described in vivid detail the sadness and tragedy of the last day of Harry Chapin's life as only he could.

And thanks too to Ben Hamper the author of what is probably one of the best books ever written about day in day out working-class life, *Rivet Head (Tales from the Assembly Line)*. Through his friend, the writer Michael Moore, Hamper got to know Harry Chapin after he came to Flint, Michigan and spent a lot of his time trying to raise money for unions.

One afternoon Josh Chapin arranged a meeting with Ben and the two of us drove the long ride from Detroit to Flint in a taxi cab to meet him in a bar. Over many drinks he told us how he watched the factories close down in Flint and how he felt the song that Harry Chapin wrote "'The Day They Closed the Factories Down' resonates clear across America."

Over the years I have had the pure good fortunate to work with some of the best editors in the New York media, some of them legendary editors who edited famous writers I looked up to before I had my own byline. And the best of them would edit my words in a way that I couldn't tell if it was edited. Naomi Rosenblatt, who edited and made suggestions for this book, is up there with them; she did the same. And I thank her for making me look good, and her suggestion to move one of the paragraphs and make it the opening line of the Introduction.

In memory, I would also like to thank the late Dennis Duggan, a writer and good friend from my days of writing freelance stories for *New York Newsday*, where he was a columnist. Taped over my writing desk are some words of guidance he wrote for me when the first miles of my journey looking for Harry Chapin's America started: "The Chapin Book Sounds Like a Fenton Affair to the Bone."

And lastly, in memory, to Pete Hamill, who encouraged me to get into the writing life a long, long time ago, after I sent him a lengthy letter in 1968 about a piece he wrote for the *Village Voice* about our old Brooklyn neighborhood called "A Melancholy Fall in the Gardens of Brooklyn." Part of his words back to me were: "Meanwhile, it's obvious from your letter that you can write like hell yourself. Why don't you do something with it?" And I did.

CPSIA information can be obtained
at www.ICGtesting.com
Printed in the USA
BVHW030217090821
613975BV00005B/202